How to Play Popular Guitar in 10 Easy Lessons

How to Play Popular Guitar in 10 Easy Lessons

Norman Monath

CONTEMPORARY BOOKS

Library of Congress Cataloging-in-Publication Data

Monath, Norman.
    How to play popular guitar in 10 easy lessons / Norman Monath.
        p.   cm.
    Includes index.
    ISBN 0-8092-3765-2
    1. Guitar—Methods—Self instruction.   I. Title.

  MT588.M78.   1994
  787.87'393—dc20   94-6522
                                      CIP
                                      MN

Guitar photos on pages 17, 21, and 23 courtesy of the Yamaha Corporation of America
and the Martin Guitar Company.
Illustrations by Kathy Dzielak on pages 30, 31, 35, 37, 41, 50, 53, and 59.
Illustrations by Todd Petersen on pages 18, 24, 27, 28, and 109.

  15 16 17 18 19 20 21 HES/HES 2 1 0 9 8 7 6 5 4

ISBN 0-8092-3765-2

McGraw-Hill books are available at special quantity discounts to use as premiums and sales
promotions, or for use in corporate training programs. For more information, please write to the
Director of Special Sales, Professional Publishing, McGraw-Hill, Two Penn Plaza, New York, NY
10121-2298. Or contact your local bookstore.

This book is printed on acid-free paper.

To Seymour Turk

Contents

Acknowledgments

To Lisa Petrusky, who encouraged me to continue working on this book, and to her husband, Eugene Brissie, who arranged to have it published.

To Hal David for permission to reprint the lead sheet of "To All the Girls I've Loved Before," which was composed by Albert Hammond, whom I thank for that beautiful song.

To Doris Chafin of the Chafin Music Center for invaluable advice about the needs of aspiring guitarists.

Above all, to Phillip J. Maragos, an excellent guitar player, and to my friends Claire Taylor, and Kirby Kooluris, and Virginia Fay, for their assistance in the preparation of the manuscript.

Preface

I studied classical guitar with Alexander Bellow, a close colleague of Andres Segovia and one of the best teachers in the world. Paul Simon—of Simon and Garfunkel—was one of his pupils, and Mr. Bellow told me that Simon was as proficient on classical guitar as he was on pop or jazz guitar.

Paul Simon didn't study the classical method until well after his success in the popular field; I, on the other hand, did just the opposite, playing the Etudes of Villa-Lobos long before attempting bluegrass or jazz. Although I have never tried to teach classical guitar, I have successfully taught a great many people how to start playing folk and popular songs within a very short time.

Also, while I was president of a division of Simon & Schuster, I published a number of guitar instruction books, thereby learning what approaches were most effective. I hope that these experiences—as well as the experience of writing a bestselling how-to book on playing the piano*—have enabled me to explain the principles of guitar playing in a simple, concise, and effective way in this book.

How to Play Popular Piano in Ten Easy Lessons (New York: Simon & Schuster, 1984)

How to Play Popular Guitar in 10 Easy Lessons

–1–
The Right Guitar for You

The violins you see today are designed almost exactly as those produced by Antonio Stradivari in the early eighteenth century. Also, the performing techniques for violin developed by the great Niccolo Paganini nearly a century later are virtually the same as those practiced today.

The history of the guitar is completely different. An offspring of the ancient oriental lute, the guitar has gone through many transformations through the years. As a matter of fact, with the advent of rock music in the 1950s and the advances in electronics, guitar manufacturers have been flooding us with innovations that are referred to as "space-age" body shapes as well as "hot-rod" paint jobs!

Nevertheless, a guitar is a guitar is a guitar: the basic elements are the same. If you can play a so-called round-hole acoustic, you can play a solid-body electric. The execution of harmonies and melodies is similar; the essential differences are in the tone qualities and volumes of the sounds. For example, even though a soprano and a tenor may be singing the very same note, your ears will easily recognize the differences in the quality of tone and volume the sounds of their voices produce. So if you have a guitar, or can borrow one, don't be concerned about what type it is as long as it has six strings. (Bass guitars, with four strings, and twelve-string guitars are not part of the group that is the subject of this book.)

If you do not have a guitar and want to know which type to choose, I offer the following suggestions: first, if you know you want to play the songs of Paul Simon, for example, or the great standards by composers of the past (Gershwin, Rodgers, Cole Porter, etc.), get a simple round-hole acoustic steel-string guitar like the one shown on page 17. This same type of guitar also will be appropriate for the songs played by such performers as Willie Nelson, Carly Simon, Dolly Parton, or the Beatles.

On the other hand, if your tastes run more along the lines of rockers such as Chuck Berry, Bruce Springsteen, or Eric Clapton (although he enjoys playing acoustic guitar, as evidenced by his album cleverly entitled *Unplugged*), then get a solid-body electric guitar. By proper use of the volume and tone controls, you can adapt the electric guitar to play country, blues, folk, and old standards as well.

One other point should be made with respect to your choice of guitars. If you're interested in acoustic models, you should not get a classical-type guitar unless you eventually intend to play classical compositions. Andres Segovia, one of the world's greatest classical guitarists (a "guitartist," if you will), could not have done justice to that style of music with anything but a classical model. Also, he had to keep the fingernails of his left hand trimmed and the nails of the middle fingers of his right hand slightly longer than normal in order to produce beautiful classical guitar tones. (You will have to keep only your left-hand nails reasonably short.)

However, if you happen to have a classical model, you can use it with this book. As a matter of fact, some beginners find it easier to position their left-hand fingers on classical guitars because they have wider necks than the other types (see page 18). The reason for this will become clear to you when you actually begin to position your left-hand fingers in Lesson 4. Nevertheless, I believe this small benefit is outweighed by other factors, particularly if you want to play only popular songs.

With a guitar, unlike most other instruments, you don't have to play each note of the melody in order to achieve a fully satisfying musical experience. This book will show you how to use what is known as a *fake book* (see Lesson 4), which may contain the melodies and chords* of over a thousand songs! You simply strum the chords while you sing or hum the melody or accompany friends who play other instruments. So even if you can't read notes, you will be able to enjoy that most rewarding musical experience: playing your favorite songs.

*Chords are created by playing several strings simultaneously or in quick enough succession to produce harmonies rather than single tones.

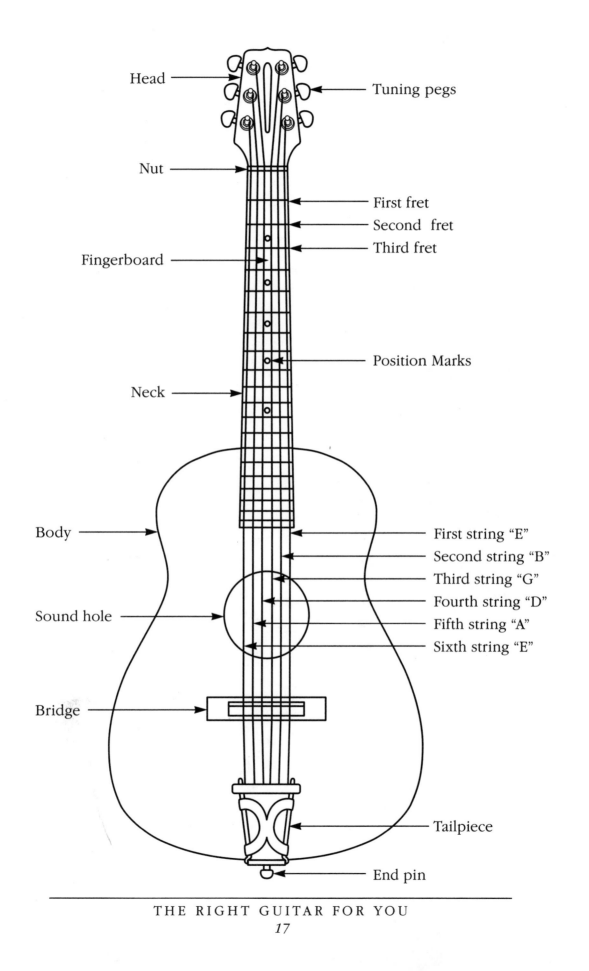

Head

Tuning pegs

Nut

First fret

Second fret

Third fret

Fingerboard

Position Marks

Neck

Body

First string "E"

Second string "B"

Third string "G"

Fourth string "D"

Sound hole

Fifth string "A"

Sixth string "E"

Bridge

Tailpiece

End pin

THE ELEMENTS OF THE GUITAR
AND THEIR FUNCTIONS

I assume you now are in possession of a guitar, acoustic or electric, similar to one of the following:

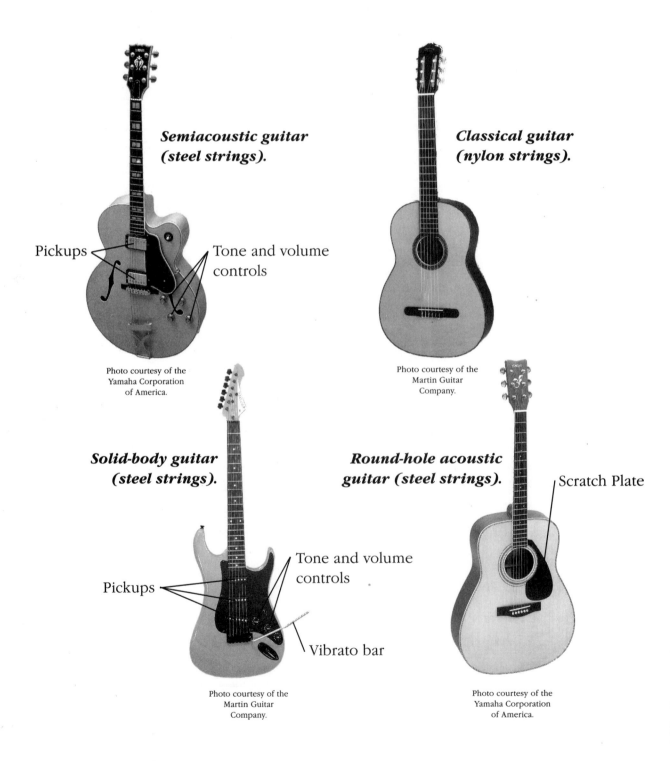

Semiacoustic guitar (steel strings).

Pickups

Tone and volume controls

Photo courtesy of the
Yamaha Corporation
of America.

Classical guitar (nylon strings).

Photo courtesy of the
Martin Guitar
Company.

Solid-body guitar (steel strings).

Pickups

Tone and volume controls

Vibrato bar

Photo courtesy of the
Martin Guitar
Company.

Round-hole acoustic guitar (steel strings).

Scratch Plate

Photo courtesy of the
Yamaha Corporation
of America.

Whether your guitar is acoustic, semiacoustic, or solid-body electric, the fundamentals are the same. An electronic keyboard, for example, looks far different from a concert grand piano. However, not only do the keys have the same names (C, D, E, etc.), but their combinations in order to form chords are also the same. So don't be concerned about the color or shape of your guitar as long as it has the essential parts as shown in the preceding illustration.

I also assume that your guitar is strung with strings that are tuned properly and are not worn out. If it is not, and if you need help in the stringing as well as the tuning of the instrument, I have provided all you need to know in the following lesson. Before that, some simple explanations of various parts of the guitar are appropriate.

The names of most of the parts of the guitar make their functions obvious: the tuning pegs are used to tighten or loosen the strings to their proper pitch; the fingerboard is where you place your fingers to form the different chords. Removable vibrato bars on electric guitars can create rapid changes, or oscillations, in pitch *simultaneously* on all six strings. If you have one, remove it at least until you've started to play some of the songs in this book.

Pickups on electric guitars pick up the vibrations of the strings and deliver them to an amplifier, where the tone and volume controls as well as the controls on the amplifier produce the desired sounds. The use and nature of pickups and the distinctions among amplifiers can be fully understood only by going to a guitar store and getting a demonstration. But these features are for the advanced guitarist, not the reader of this book.

Strictly speaking, *frets* are the horizontal metal ridges that lie across the fingerboard and under the strings. However, for all practical purposes it is best to think of frets as being the *spaces* between the ridges. This is because of the way chord diagrams are designed. *Chord diagrams* indicate the placement of the left-hand fingers. They consist of vertical lines representing the six strings and horizontal lines representing the ridges. For example, the diagram of a chord in which fingers are to be placed on the first fret of the third string, the second fret of the fourth string, and the second fret of the fifth string might look like this:

Strings

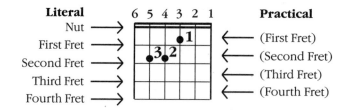

The left side of the diagram shows frets as they are actually defined. The right side shows how you would read a diagram for all practical purposes. You can see why it is preferable to think of frets as being the spaces rather than the ridges.

The numbers 1, 2, and 3 next to the finger-placement marks specify which fingers to use (see page 35). When you see no fret numbers, you can assume that the top line represents the nut and the top space represents the first fret. Also, frets are referred to as *higher* as they become farther from the nut and closer to the bridge.

For chords in which finger placements begin on somewhat high frets, the diagrams are simplified so that a large portion of the fingerboard doesn't have to be shown. For example, if finger placement for a particular chord happens to begin on the tenth fret, a chord diagram might be drawn in either of these ways:

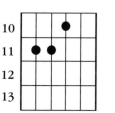   OR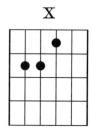

Otherwise, these chord diagrams would be as long as this:

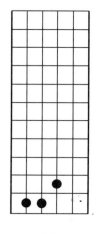

Obviously, this is impractical as well as a waste of space, even if all the diagrammed frets were numbered for the benefit of quick location.

There is no need to fret any further about frets (I couldn't resist that!), so let's move on to position marks. These allow your eyes to quickly determine where a particular fret is located. The usual locations for position marks are on the third, fifth, seventh, ninth, and twelfth frets on acoustic guitars. (Electric guitars, which have longer fingerboards, have additional position marks.) Thus, if a chord diagram begins on the tenth fret, you can spot it immediately on the guitar because it is next to the ninth position mark.

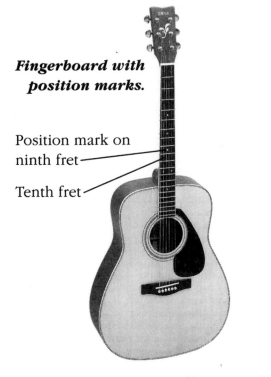

Fingerboard with position marks.

Position mark on ninth fret

Tenth fret

Photo courtesy of the
Yamaha Corporation
of America.

Fingerboard without position marks (classical guitars do not have position marks).

Photo courtesy of the
Martin Guitar
Company.

—2—
Guitar Strings and Tuning

There are two main types of guitar strings: nylon and steel. Nylon strings must be used on classical guitars. They are also used on flamenco guitars, which are used mainly for the kind of Spanish music that involves thumping on the body of the instrument. A scratch plate, or finger guard, protects the flamenco guitar from being scratched.

Scratch Plate

Photo courtesy of the Yamaha Corporation of America.

Most steel-string guitars now have scratch plates because their bodies are often vulnerable to scratches from picks, especially when the music being played is rock 'n' roll. A pick is usually a thin piece of plastic in the shape of an isosceles triangle:

A guitar pick.

Picks are rarely used on nylon strings, not only because of the kind of music nylons are meant for but because the texture of nylon strings isn't strong enough to withstand the scraping. Also, nylons are never used on electric guitars for the same reason—their texture. If used purely acoustically, they might survive on an electric body for the kinder, gentler variety of folk, pop, blues, and country music; but hooked up to an amplifier for soft—let alone, hard—rock? Forget it! Besides producing an anemic sound, they'd bust in a minute.

Nylon strings come in different degrees of tension, varying from very low to very high. Advanced classical guitarists prefer those of highest tension because the strings respond more quickly to the stroking of the fingers. Steel strings come in different gauges (thicknesses) and also may be wound differently. For example, you can find everything from ultralight-gauge silver-plated strings to heavy-gauge bronze-wound strings. For beginners, medium-gauge, regular-wound steel strings are best. (New sets of strings are individually packaged so that you know which string is first, second, third, etc.) However, start with whatever you happen to have available.

TUNING YOUR GUITAR

The vibrations of the strings are what determine their pitch, and those vibrations occur between the nut and the bridge. The distance between the nut and the bridge as well as the tension of the strings combine to create the pitches produced. Tension is controlled by turning the tuning pegs to tighten or loosen the strings. Distance is shortened or lengthened by the left-hand fingers. When you press a finger on a fret you are actually creating a new nut, thereby shortening the length of the string. And when you shorten the length of a string you are raising the pitch.

The following diagram shows the notes to which the six strings are tuned and how they correspond to the notes of a piano:

Now that one end of the string is in place, bring the other end to the proper tuning peg mechanism.

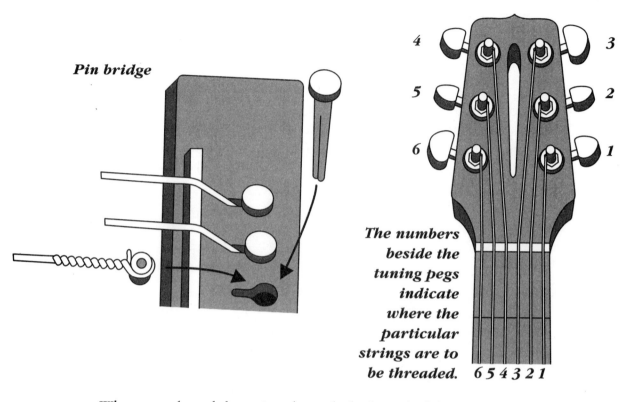

Pin bridge

The numbers beside the tuning pegs indicate where the particular strings are to be threaded. 6 5 4 3 2 1

When you thread the string through the barrel of the tuning peg, you have to loop it underneath itself to keep it from slipping. I do this by holding the end of the string away from the head of the guitar so that when I turn the peg *counterclockwise* a few times, the string will be winding around itself enough to stay firmly in place. Be sure to fit the string over the proper groove in the nut.

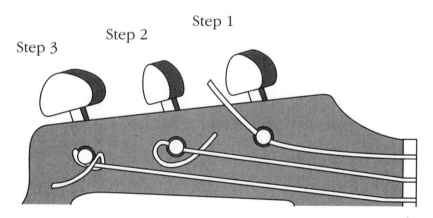

Step 1

Step 2

Step 3

Loop a string under and then over itself to secure it to the barrel of the tuning machine.

I recommend at first tuning a string slightly higher in pitch than called for. The reason is simply that newly strung strings have a tendency to stretch after a while. You will probably find that your newly overtightened strings will slip into tune by themselves after a few hours.

The process of connecting nylon strings to a classical or Spanish-type bridge is different from what I described above. Your strings won't be balled at one end, although they may have a knot at one end. Even so, you may not be able to depend on the knot to keep the string from slipping through the hole of the bridge. I sometimes cut off the knot and wind the string under and over itself about three times to keep it from slipping.

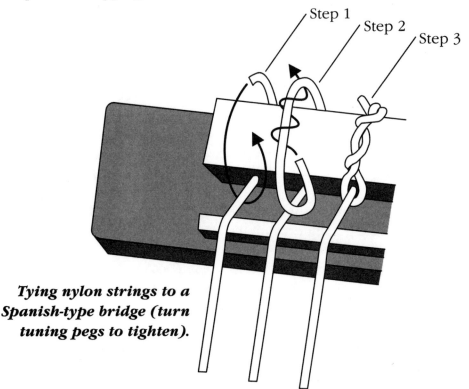

Tying nylon strings to a Spanish-type bridge (turn tuning pegs to tighten).

After you have finished the restringing, cut the ends of the strings down to no more than a few extra inches so they don't dangle all over the place. Steel strings projecting from the head of a guitar can be dangerous to your eyes.

—3—
Holding the Guitar

There are five basic ways to hold a guitar, three of which are in a sitting position (see page 30). The position I recommend for the beginner (and my favorite way) is simply sitting, legs uncrossed, with the guitar resting on the right leg.

A variant of this position is to cross the right leg over the left. This position has been described as "casual," "relaxed," or "informal." However, I find it tiring after about five minutes (one leg usually falls asleep), so I don't recommend it.

The classical sitting position involves the use of a small guitar footstool under the left leg, elevating it about five or six inches. The guitar then rests on the left leg. Since we are not concerned with learning classical music in this book I suggest either of the first two sitting positions, even if you happen to have a classical model.

An important point with respect to any of the sitting positions is to sit on a chair without arms and on a firm surface. Don't try sitting in the middle of a sofa or on the edge of a bed. You might find your left elbow touching the surfaces of those seats, and that won't allow you enough freedom in positioning your fingers.

The left hand should not be used to hold the guitar in *any* of the sitting positions. Just as a violinist can remove his or her left hand from the fingerboard without having the instrument fall from its position between the chin and collarbone, you also should be able to remove your left hand from your guitar without affecting its position.

The two remaining positions are simply standing with or without a guitar strap to hold the guitar. Some performers like to elevate the right leg on a stool or a low chair so that the guitar can rest on the right leg.

POSITIONING THE HANDS AND FINGERS

In the starting position, the right-hand fingers should be at right angles to the strings; the thumb is more or less parallel to the strings. The right forearm, wrist, and fingers should be reasonably loose. The thumb and forefinger of the left hand should be parallel to each other and form a "U" when viewed from the side; the remaining fingers should be slightly curved.

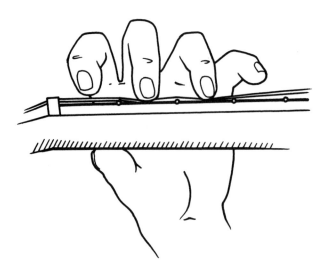

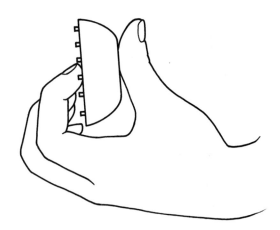

The thumb and forefinger of the left hand should be parallel and form a "U" shape.

A side view of the "U" position.

Try the following exercise while holding the guitar in the proper starting position. Without actually touching the neck and fingerboard with your left hand, position your fingers over the first fret, as shown here:

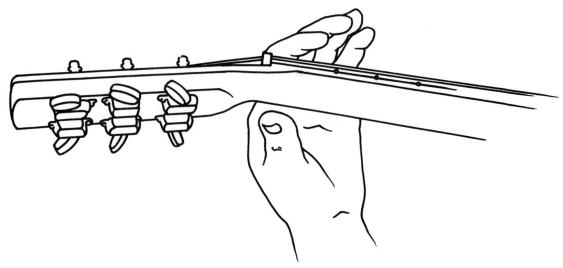

Note that the forefinger is at, or nearly at, right angles to the strings, and the ball of the thumb is under the middle of the neck. (I say "nearly at" because over the first, second, or third frets it is more difficult to achieve a true right angle than it is over the higher frets.) Move your left hand over to one of the higher frets—the ninth, for example—and you will undoubtedly find it much easier to achieve a true right angle. The more you play, the easier it will be for you to get a reasonable right angle on the lower frets; this will come in handy when you try to play certain chords.

Next, press the first fret firmly with your forefinger and the neck with your thumb. Now use your right-hand thumb to strike each string with a downward motion, and see if you produce a musical tone on each string, from the sixth to the first. If you are getting fuzzy sounds, it may be because you're not pressing the strings firmly enough with your forefinger, or maybe your forefinger isn't close enough to the first ridge. (Remember—I use the word *fret* to refer to the spaces rather than the ridges.)

After positioning your left-hand forefinger so that you can produce a clear tone on each string, move to the second fret, then to the third, and so on, as high up the neck as you can go. Before you move to a higher fret, be sure to produce clear tones on each of the strings without having to press too strongly. By being firm as well as relaxed, you won't end up with finger fatigue.

When you use your forefinger over all the strings of a fret in this way, you are creating what is called a *bar*. (If you see the word *barré* in a guitar book, it means the same thing.) The bar position is very useful in creating different chords. And the more you do this bar exercise the easier it will be for you to play any other chord forms.

Bar chords may be diagrammed in the following ways:

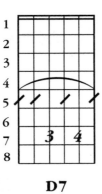

D7

OR

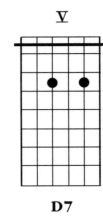

D7

Form the bar on the fifth fret and place the third and fourth fingers on the seventh fret.

The solid line represents a bar on the fifth fret, producing the same chord as that shown on the left.

−4−
First Chords, Strums, and Songs

Near the end of the first lesson, I indicated that you do not have to play the specific notes of the melodies of your favorite songs. Most amateur guitarists strum the harmonies—the chords, that is—and find that to be a fully satisfying musical experience. Although the aim of this book is to teach you how to do just that, I have provided an appendix for those who want to be able to read notes and play melodies.

At this point, I am assuming that you would like to start playing whether or not you know one note from another. Further, I assume that you don't know what strings to strike in order to produce the right harmonies but that you have, or at some point later are willing to get, the sheet music to the songs of your choice or a fake book, which I will tell you about in this lesson.

So, suppose you wanted to play "Silent Night." In the usual popular sheet-music form, it might begin like the sample on the following page.

As you can see, notes are written on horizontal lines and spaces called *staffs*. Most sheet music consists of three staffs (sometimes called *staves*), the lower two of which are bracketed and represent the notes for the piano. The lowest staff shows the notes for the pianist's left hand, and the middle staff shows the notes for the right hand. The top staff is called the vocal line because singers use it for the melody and words.

Silent Night

Slowly

The vocal line not only shows the melody and words but the harmonies as well. For example, above the first word of "Silent Night" you can see the letter C, and above the word "All" you can see G7. Those letters are referred to as guitar chords although they can be used by any instrument capable of playing chords, such as an organ or any type of keyboard. As a matter of fact, the two lower staves are often ignored by pianists who choose to play the melody using a C chord and a G7 chord that they form in their own way. Piano parts in popular sheet music are rarely even written by the composers of the songs. They usually simply write the vocal line, leaving it to whomever the music publisher hires to arrange the piano part. The vocal line, when it appears by itself, is generally called a *lead* (pronounced "leed") sheet.

Since most musicians need only the lead sheet of a song in order to play it, they don't buy relatively expensive sheet music, they buy so-called fake books, which contain just the lead sheets indicating the words, melodies, and harmonies. The space thus saved makes it possible for a single fake book to carry a thousand or more songs! You will find fake books invaluable once you know how to read them.

Now you are ready to learn how to play some chords and how to strum them for your first songs. Once you can do this, you will be able to play from sheet music, fake books, or even by ear. If all you know is the melody of a song, you can just start strumming, humming, and before you know it the right chords will start coming!

CHORD DIAGRAMS

In chord diagrams, the fingers are numbered as follows:

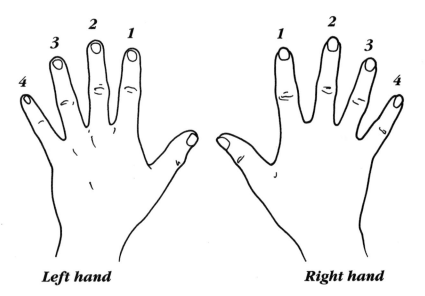

Left hand   **Right hand**

Thus, the forefinger is referred to as the *first* finger, the middle finger as the *second* finger, and so on. For example, here are four ways to diagram a C chord:

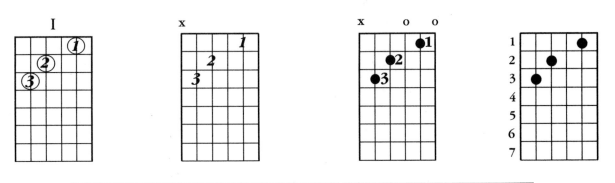

All of these diagrams tell you to press the first fret of the second string with your first finger, the second fret of the fourth string with your second finger, and the third fret of the fifth string with your third finger. The first three diagrams specify which fingers to use; the fourth doesn't.

Although you can always assume that the top fret of a diagram represents the first fret when no number is shown above or alongside, as in the second and third diagrams, you may see a Roman numeral I, as in the first diagram. Also, the *o*'s above the first and third strings in the third diagram stand for *open* strings. That means those strings are part of the chord and should be strummed. The *x*'s above the second and third diagrams mean that you should not strum the sixth string but begin with your thumb or pick on the fifth string.

Since the first and fourth diagrams from the preceding page have no *o* or *x* indications, the implication is that you begin by first striking the highest *marked* string and continue striking all the rest in a downward direction. The following examples indicate that you should strike only the fourth, third, second, and first strings:

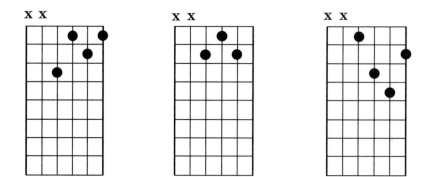

These three diagrams as well as the fourth C-chord diagram from the preceding page show no numbers for the fingers. That's because in most cases you won't be able to use any *but* the correct fingers. Besides, some people may choose alternative fingering because of the particular physical attributes of their hands and/or fingers. However, I strongly urge you to use the fingering specified for the chords you are about to learn.

The following illustrations show how the C and G7 chords are most often diagrammed and how they are fingered.

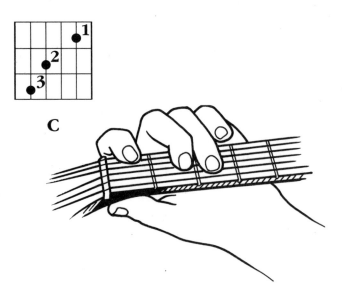

C

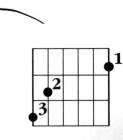

G7

FIRST CHORDS AND STRUMS

We will begin with the C chord: First, press only your first finger on the first fret of the second string. With a gentle, downward stroke of your right thumb *brush* both the second and first strings, one right after the other. If you are getting a fuzzy, nonmusical sound from the second string, press more firmly with your first left-hand finger or move it closer to the first ridge or, if necessary, do both.

When executing this simple thumb strum, you may find it comfortable to rest the other fingers of your right hand on the surface of the guitar. Doing this will result in a gentler thumb strum because you won't have a tendency to add the force of your forearm. Also, your fingers will be in a better position to change to a different type of strum.

Continue this procedure by adding your second finger to the second fret of the fourth string and strumming all four strings. When you are satisfied with the sound, complete the C chord by adding your third finger to the third fret of the fifth string.

This C chord requires you to strike all but the sixth string. The G7 chord involves all six strings, as you can see from the diagram. Once you've mastered the C chord, follow the same procedure in learning the G7 chord.

You are now ready to alternate playing the C and G7 chords, one after the other, until you can change from one to the other in a reasonable amount of time. ("Reasonable" at this stage means within four or five seconds.) Eventually, you will be able to make the changes immediately. Not lifting your left-hand fingers too high between the chord changes, for example, will greatly facilitate your finger movements. Also, if you carefully observe which fingers move where, you will be better prepared and will find it easier to relax your wrist and fingers. Relaxation is one of the most important keys to changing chord positions. Above all, don't be discouraged now if it seems to take you a long time to change back and forth from C to G7. Set your own comfortable pace, but be sure that you are fingering the chords firmly enough to produce gratifying tones.

Knowing just the C and G7 chords makes it possible for you to begin to play numerous songs. I have chosen three easy ones and have marked the chords over the words or syllables to indicate when those chords should be strummed. You should play them at a tempo that is comfortable for you.

For singing the words or simply humming, the first note of all three of these songs is C. One of the easiest ways to find this note is to play the note C on a keyboard if you have one and know the letter designations of the keys. Another way is to strum the C and G7 chords and find it by ear. Some people can do that easily, but if you can't, don't worry about it. It's a skill you will eventually develop unless you are tone-deaf, in which case you would not have begun reading this book.

Yet another way to find the C, or any other note, is to strum it on the guitar; that's the way I have chosen to guide you in the following songs. Thus, to find C, press the third fret of the fifth string with your third finger—strumming that string will produce a C. To find the note E, you can simply strum either the first or sixth open strings. The first string will produce a much higher E than the sixth string, but you will have found the *pitch* of the note E and can at least have a useful guide in accommodating your voice.

Clementine

Starting note: C (third fret of fifth string)

Thumb strum: Strum the chord once, only on the word or syllable indicated.

    C   **C**   **C**   **G7**
In a cav—ern, in a can—yon, ex—ca—va—ting for a mine,

     G7   **C**   **G7**   **C**
Lived a min—er, for—ty nin—er, and his daugh—ter, Clem—en—tine.

     C   **C**   **C**   **G7**
Oh, my dar—ling, oh, my dar—ling, oh, my dar—ling, Clem—en—tine,

     G7   **C**   **G7**   **C**
You are lost and gone for—ev—er, dread—ful sor—ry, Clem—en—tine.

When a song is in the key of C, this means that the C chord represents "home plate," so to speak. In other words, the sound of the C chord is the sound the song can end on—the tension created by any other chords that may have preceded it has been released or resolved by the sound of the C chord. For example, when you played the C and G7 chords alternately in "Clementine," you may have noticed that the G7 seemed to create a feeling of anticipation, a feeling of waiting for the other shoe to drop, and that when you played the C chord you felt a sense of resolution.

When you use the C and G7 chords to play "Clementine," you are playing the song in the key of C. If I wanted you to play it in the key of G, for example, I would have shown you the diagrams for D7 and G, and your ear would have accepted the G chord as the chord of resolution. Further, the first note of "Clementine" in the key of C happens to be C. (I say *happens* because songs don't always begin on the first note of the key in which they are written. Although they can begin on almost any note, they almost always end on C if they are played in the key of C, or G if played in the key of G, etc.) Since the tune of "Clementine" begins on C when played in that key, it would begin on G if you played it in the key of G.

So if the key of C is not best for your voice on these first three songs, you will soon enough be able to use different chords (D7 and G or E7 and A) to suit your voice. As a matter of fact, in Lesson 6 you will learn how to play "Clementine" with the A and E7 chords instead of the C and G7 chords.

The next song, "Skip to My Lou," provides an opportunity to learn a different strum—I call it the thumb bass and brush. When playing the C chord, starting with your thumb on the fifth string; don't brush all the downward strings but let your thumb stop on the fourth string. Then continue by doing the simple thumb strum on the fourth, third, second, and first strings. By coming to rest on the fourth string, only the fifth string will be sounded, providing the *bass* part of the strum since it is the lowest note. Then when you continue the strum starting on the fourth string, you are providing the *brush* part.

In this song, when you see a chord letter, do just the bass part; do the following brush part when you see a ✓ mark. When you play the G7 chord, strum the *sixth* string and brush the rest.

Skip to My Lou

Starting note: E (second fret of fourth string)

Thumb Bass and Brush Strum: Thumb strums one string on the chord letter and brushes on the check mark. A dash (——) after a word means that you should hold that word while you follow the strumming indication(s) above the dash.

C ✓   C   ✓ C ✓ C ✓
Flies in the but—ter milk shoo fly shoo,——

G7 ✓   G7   ✓ G7 ✓ G7 ✓
Flies in the but—ter milk shoo fly shoo,——

C ✓   C   ✓ C ✓ C ✓
Flies in the but—ter milk shoo fly shoo,——

G7 ✓   G7 ✓ C ✓ C C*
Skip to my Lou my dar—ling.——

*On the last C chord you may strum *all* five strings briskly to give the song a socko ending.

The next song, "Row, Row, Row Your Boat," involves another kind of strum—the thumb bass and pluck. This one begins in exactly the same way as the thumb bass and brush: in playing a C chord, for example, you strike the fifth string with your thumb, letting it come to rest when it touches the fourth string. Now, however, instead of brushing the remaining strings with your thumb, you pluck them simultaneously with your first three fingers.

When you start this strum for the C chord with your thumb on the fifth string, you may rest your first finger on the third string, your second finger on the second string, and your third finger on the first string. The following diagram shows that starting position:

Thumb rests on fifth string.

First finger rests on third string.

Second finger rests on second string.

Third finger rests on first string.

After strumming the fifth string on the first beat, you then pluck the other three strings on the next beat. (The term *beat* will be explained in detail in the next lesson.) In "Row, Row, Row Your Boat," do the thumb bass strum on the chord letter and pluck on the ✓ mark.

Row, Row, Row Your Boat

Starting note: C (third fret of fifth string)

Thumb Bass and Pluck Strum: Thumb strums one string on chord letter; other fingers pluck on ✓ mark.

C　✓　**C**　✓　**C**　✓　　　**C**　✓
Row,—row,—row—your boat—

　C　✓　**C**　✓　　　**C**　✓　**C**　✓
Gent—ly down—the stream.— — —

　C　✓　**C**　✓　**C**　✓　**C**　✓
Merr—i—ly, merr—i—ly, merr—i—ly, merr—i—ly,

G7 ✓　**G7** ✓　　**C**　✓ **C***
Life—is but—a dream.—

*Here again, as at the end of the last song, you may execute a final, emphatic thumb strum signifying the ending.

—5—
Rhythm, Note Values, and Rests

In this book the word *rhythm* refers to a series of accents, or beats, that occur at regular, or equal, time intervals. For example, if you were to clap your hands once each second, counting ONE, two, three, four, ONE, two, three, four, and accenting each number-one clap, you would be establishing a four-beat rhythmic pattern. If you counted three beats—ONE, two, three, ONE, two, three, etc.—instead of four, you would be establishing a three-beat rhythmic pattern. The four-beat rhythm is called *duple* since it is divisible by two, and the three-beat rhythm is called *triple*. The songs you will be learning in this book are written in duple or triple time.

Guitar strums establish different rhythmic patterns. In order for you to follow them correctly, it is helpful to understand the *time values* of notes.

A whole note on a music staff looks like this:

Its exact location on the staff simply defines what note it is (in these examples, a C and a B) but does not affect its time value. That is determined by the number of beats it represents as well as how slowly or quickly the particular music is to be played. For example, a whole note representing four beats in a slow song will be sustained longer than four beats in a fast song with shorter intervals between the beats. Look at the following excerpts:

Swing Low, Sweet Chariot

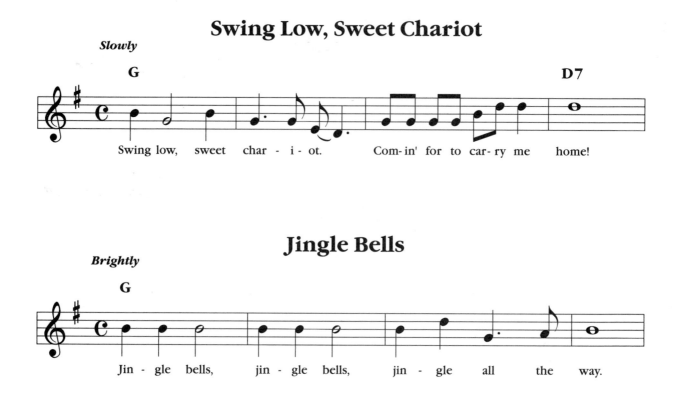

Jingle Bells

The whole notes appear at the end of each line—above the words "home!" and "way." There are also half notes, which look like whole notes with stems (♩); they appear above the word "low" in the first example and above "bells" in the second.

If you sing these excerpts, I'm sure you will notice that you hold the word "home!" longer than you hold the word "way." You also will find yourself holding the word "low" longer than "bells," even though both are given half-note values. So even though the whole notes each have four beats and the half notes each have two in these examples, their duration depends upon the rapidity of the beats and not on what kind of notes they are.

A *measure*, sometimes called a *bar*, consists of a specific number of note values or beats. Measures are separated by bar lines. (Thus, the words "Jin—gle all the" are in the third measure.) Each individual measure in both examples contains four beats. We know this because of "C" at the beginning of the first measures. That symbol stands for *common* time, sometimes written as 4/4 and often referred to as *four-quarter* time, meaning that a quarter note gets one beat. Quarter notes are the black notes with stems (♩) that you see above the syllables of "Jin—gle." Since each measure has the value of four quarter notes, a whole note will get all four beats, a half note will get two, and eighth

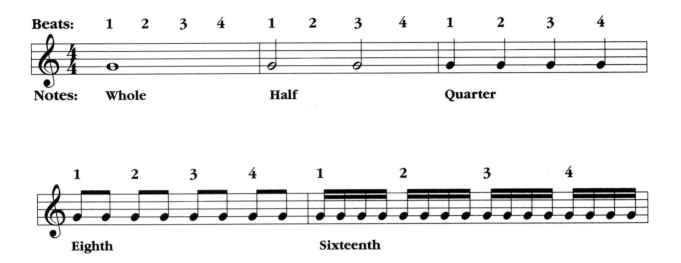

notes (♪♪ or ♫) will get a half beat (meaning two eighth notes to one beat).

Dots are used to extend the duration of notes by half their original value. Thus, a dotted half note (♩.) would be equal to three quarter notes (♩♩♩); a dotted quarter note would equal three eighths (♪♪♪).

Rests are periods of silence and have the same duration (number of beats) as the notes that correspond to their values. Dotting them has the same effect as dotting notes—their value increases by one-half.

-      Whole rest
-      Half rest
- ♩   Quarter rest
- ♪   Eighth rest
- ♪   Sixteenth rest

Notes also may be extended in their time value by being tied:

The dotted half note in the second measure is worth three quarter notes. By being tied by the curved line to the same notes in the third and fourth measures, its value has been increased to a total of seven quarters. When notes are tied in this way, they are not played again but simply held for the appropriate amount of time. When curved lines appear between *different* notes, as in the vocal line of "Silent Night,"

on page 34, they are called *slurs* and are not treated like ties. Slurs indicate that those notes are to be played as a single unit: one up or down stroke on a violin, one breath on a woodwind instrument, or legato on a piano. (*Legato* means to play successive notes smoothly, without perceptible interruption.)

The effect of a dotted note is generally to "make room" for a musical tone that occurs after or before the regular beat in a particular measure. Instead of just containing four quarter notes, a measure in 4/4 time could contain a half note plus two quarter notes or a dotted half note followed by *one* quarter note. The dotted half note is the equivalent of three quarter notes, so adding another quarter note fulfills the value of the measure.

For example, look at the second measure of the excerpt of "Swing Low, Sweet Chariot," as shown below. The time signature of that song indicates four beats to each measure and a total note value of four quarters. The first note is a dotted quarter, worth three eighths. Next is an eighth, followed by another eighth and a dotted quarter. The measure adds up to a total value of four quarters; but how do the dotted notes affect the beats with regard to strumming?

Simple thumb strum:

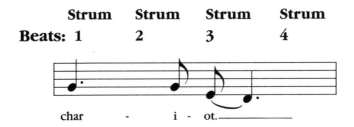

Note that the second beat occurs after the first syllable of "chariot" and the fourth beat occurs after the last note. Clap your hands four times, slowly, and sing "chariot" as you would sing it normally, and you'll observe the effect of the first note being a dotted quarter. If that measure were written without any dotted notes, the same beats and strums would occur as follows:

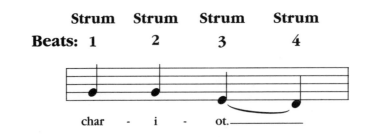

Performing it in this way would sound very unmusical, particularly since we're used to hearing it as normally played. (The curved line under the last two notes of the word "chariot" is a slur, indicating that those two notes are meant to cover the final syllable, "-ot.")

As you now know, four quarter notes are the equivalent of eight eighths as well as sixteen sixteenths. Since most music is written in terms of quarter-note values, and there are four quarter notes to a measure in 4/4 (or C) time, most people think in terms of four beats. If you wanted to think in terms of eighths and still have four beats, you could count from one to eight and accent the first, third, fifth, and seventh numbers—that would still give you four beats. For example:

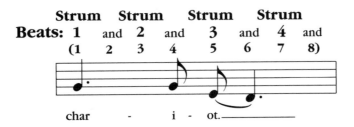

Using "and" enhances the feeling of four beats to a bar.

There are times when it is helpful to explicitly recognize eight pulses though still sticking to four beats. That is done by counting "one and, two and, three and, four and" instead of counting from one to eight.

The relevance of this lesson will become clear to you later if it isn't right now. So don't worry about any technicalities that are not perfectly clear. In any case, you now are ready to learn two important new chords that will enable you to play many, many more songs.

—6—
New Chords, New Keys, New Strums

The A and E7 chords relate to each other the same way as do the C and G7 chords. In Lesson 4 you learned that when you play the C and G7 chords, the G7 chord creates a feeling of tension that is resolved when followed by the C chord. The note C itself became a sort of "home plate" to the ear in that context, and when any note becomes the note of resolution we say we are playing in the key designated by that note. Thus, playing C and G7 chords a number of times, one after the other, establishes the key of C.

Similarly, when you play the A and E7 chords alternately, you will find that you are playing in the key of A because the A chord, or the note A by itself, will have become home plate. These are the diagrams for the A and E7 chords:

A   **E7**

Begin to finger these chords with your left hand following the same procedure that you used learning the C and G7 chords. Because for the A chord the positions of your second, third, and fourth fingers are all on the same fret, you won't be able to keep them parallel to the surrounding ridges. Instead, you will find it necessary to slant the position of your fingers so that your second finger is slightly closer to the first ridge than the third finger is and the fourth finger is the closest to the second ridge.

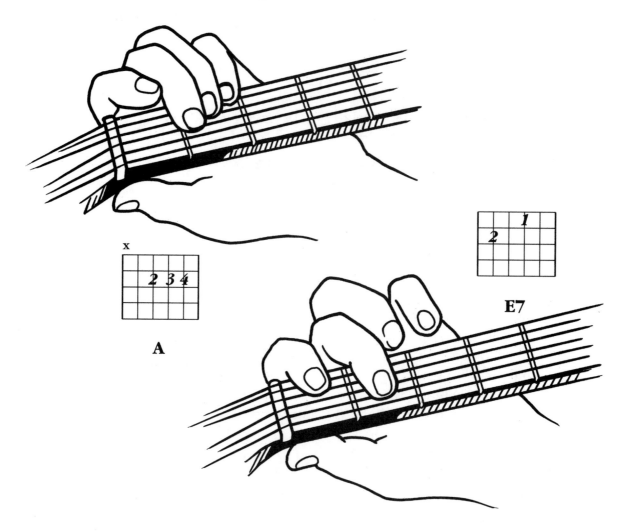

The E7 chord is one of the easiest two-fingered chords to play, and because it involves all six strings as well as the notes to which the open strings are tuned, it produces a luscious sound.

CHANGING KEYS

After you have played the A and E7 chords so that you can strum them alternately at a reasonable pace, start to use them in the first song you learned, "Clementine." Instead of the C chord, you will now play the A chord, and the E7 chord will substitute for the G7 chord. Use the same simple thumb strum that you started with, strumming only where the chord letter appears, and find the proper starting note as indicated.

Clementine

Starting note: A (open fifth string or second fret of third string)

Thumb strum: Strum once only on the word (or syllable) indicated.

A   **A**   **A**   **E7**
In a cav—ern, in a can—yon, ex—ca—va—ting for a mine,

    E7   **A**   **E7**   **A**
Lived a min—er, for—ty nin—er, and his daugh—ter, Clem—en—tine.

    A   **A**   **A**   **E7**
Oh, my dar—ling, oh, my dar—ling, oh, my dar—ling, Clem—en—tine,

    E7   **A**   **E7**   **A**
You are lost and gone for—ev—er, dread—ful sor—ry, Clem—en—tine.

You can now play "Clementine" in two keys. If you wanted to play it in the next higher key, you could form a bar with your first finger and duplicate the A and E7 chord positions:

F7

E7 chord position with bar becomes F7 chord.

B♭

The A chord position with bar becomes B♭ chord.

From these diagrams you can see that the relative positions of your fingers are the same for the B♭ and F7 chords as for the A and E7 chords. You have raised the pitch from A to B♭ by forming a bar, thereby creating a new nut. This bar chord for the F7 is probably easy for you to do at this time; however, the B♭ bar chord may be difficult because the frets closest to the neck are longer than the higher ones. It might be easier for you to form a barred A position if you place your second, third, and fourth fingers first and then create the bar with your first finger on the appropriate fret.

Try the A chord position with the bar on the fifth fret:

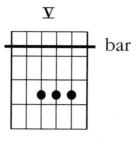

D

***The A chord position becomes D chord
because of the bar on the fifth fret.***

The A chord becomes a B♭ chord when the bar is on the first fret and
becomes a D chord when the bar is on the fifth fret because the progression of notes is A, B♭, B, C, C♯, D, etc. This progression is fully explained in the Appendix for those who wish to learn how to read notes.
For now, the essential point is that you see the notes progressing from
A to D and understand the effect of a bar on the *key* of a chord.

To demonstrate this pattern further, try the following the E7 chord
position with the bar on the fifth fret:

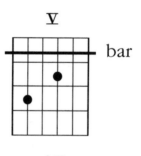

A7

***E7 chord position becomes A7 chord
because of the bar on the fifth fret.***

The progression of chord letters from E7 to A7 is F7, F♯7, G7, G♯7,
and A7. Notes in music are designated by only seven letters of the al-
phabet—A, B, C, D, E, F, and G—and this E7 chord progression follows
that sequence: E, F, G, and then A. (The reason for the ♯ chords in between is explained in the Appendix.)

Some bar chords can be extremely awkward for your left-hand fingers to form, so a *capo* may be a handy device to have, especially when
playing certain kinds of music, such as bluegrass. A capo is simply a
device that forms a bar *mechanically*, which gives you the freedom to

---

use your first finger to press any fret. There are various types of capos—some are made of elastic materials and some are made of metals.

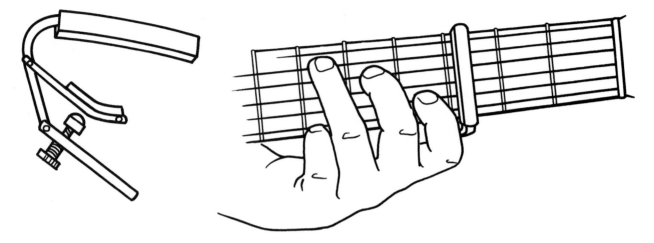

A metallic spring capo.

With the capo on the third fret the* C *chord position becomes an* E♭ *chord.

A capo and a bar both allow you to raise the pitches of the various chords. Furthermore, if you make a capo or bar move up the frets with a major chord or a seventh chord, it will remain the same kind of major or seventh chord except for its change of pitch. In other words, if it was a dominant seventh as opposed to a minor seventh, it would remain as a dominant seventh: G7 to A7, for example, and not G7 to Am7 (A "minor" 7).

The fact that you can change the pitches of chords with a capo or a bar means that you can change a song from one key to another without knowing how to read music. Thus, if you're playing a song using chords that make the melody too high or too low for your voice or for any singer or group you are accompanying, as long as you know how to form those chords you can raise or lower them without having to change your finger positions. Of course, the more chords you know the less important it becomes to have to rely on a capo.

BASIC FIRST CHORDS

In the following chord diagrams a letter by itself, as in the first chord or fourth chord, means that it is a *major* chord. It could have been written with an *M* for *major*—as CM or DM, for example—but in the case of simple major chords the single letter designation is sufficient.

A lowercase *m* stands for *minor*. Thus, the 9th chord is a simple A minor chord; the 14th is an A minor seventh.

The other seventh chords diagrammed here are known as *dominant* sevenths. The G7 chord, for example, is the chord of tension in the key of C, as you have learned. Because it creates this feeling of anticipation, its harmony is said to be "dominant" with respect to the C chord. Thus, G7 is actually G dominant seventh; but for the sake of brevity all dominant sevenths are designated G7, A7, C7, etc.

The distinctions between the various chords (major seventh, minor seventh, suspended seventh, etc.) are explained in more detail in the Appendix if you wish to learn more about them. For now, you should practice these common basic chords, playing all strings not marked with an *x*.

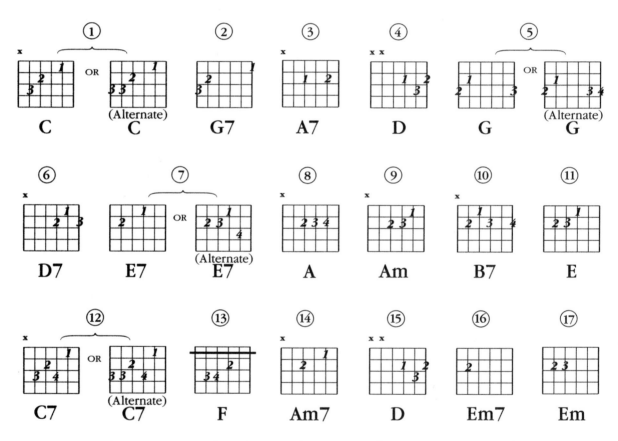

As you can see, there is sometimes more than one way to produce a certain chord. Although the basic harmony will be the same, there will be differences in sound because some strings will be playing higher or lower notes that make up that particular chord. For example, the lowest C on a standard eighty-eight-key piano is the third white key from the left. But there are seven other Cs on the standard piano, and building the same chord on some of the higher Cs will result in a different quality of sound, although those chords will have the same *named* notes. Similarly, you can play different C chords on a guitar and get differing qualities of the sound.

Being able to change sound quality by playing the same chord in different positions allows you greater mobility. If, for example, you have to follow an E chord with a B7 in a certain song, you may benefit from being able to choose the E chord position that makes it easier to change to the particular form of B7 you want to hear.

FINGERPICKING

In "Auld Lang Syne," (page 58) your next song, you will use four chords instead of only two, and you will learn to read the chord symbols from a lead sheet like those you will find in sheet music and fake books instead of just from the lyrics. By reading from a lead sheet it will become clear that chord symbols remain in effect until changed by the appearance of a different symbol. If you were using a simple thumb strum, for example, you could strum the G chord at the beginning once, on the first and third beats, or even on all four beats until you change to the D7 in the second measure.

Note that the D7 chord symbol is in the *second* measure. That's because the measures are counted from the double bar lines at the beginning rather than from the first word, "Should." That first word—actually, the first note above it—is called a *pickup*. The true beginning of a song is considered to be where the first main accent occurs. For example, the first two words of "Clementine," "In a," are pickups. You may not always see double bar lines follow pickups. Technically, they should, as in the case of "To All the Girls I've Loved Before," (page 72), in which the first five words are pickups and are followed by double bar lines.

In "Auld Lang Syne" you also will learn a new style of strumming—*fingerpicking*—and will learn about tablature in the process. The fingerpicking style we will start with is similar to the thumb bass and pluck strum except that instead of plucking strings one, two, and three simultaneously, you pluck them one after the other. When strings are plucked one after the other, they are actually being played as *arpeggios* rather than as chords—the first movement of Beethoven's "Moonlight Sonata," for example, is written in arpeggio style. However, the term *fingerpicking* seems more appropriate for the guitar.

The simplest way to describe the easy fingerpicking style you will begin with is to write it out in *tablature*. A relatively primitive form of music notation that probably originated in the fifteenth century, tablature usually accompanies music for the lute family of instruments but was often used for keyboard instruments. Bach (1685–1750) sometimes used it. In modern times it is used mainly for those who cannot read music as normally written but who know which guitar string is which and can also count the frets. The six lines of tablature represent the six strings, and the circled numbers on the lines specify the frets of the particular strings. (Sometimes the numbers designating the frets may not be circled, particularly when open strings are specified.) For example, a G chord in tablature, or TAB, would appear as follows:

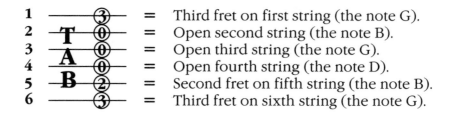

1 ③	=	Third fret on first string (the note G).
2 ⑥	=	Open second string (the note B).
3 ⑥	=	Open third string (the note G).
4 ⑥	=	Open fourth string (the note D).
5 ②	=	Second fret on fifth string (the note B).
6 ③	=	Third fret on sixth string (the note G).

The G chord is made up of the notes G, B, and D, so striking the strings in these TAB specifications would produce the G chord. Here is the equivalent chord diagram:

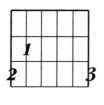

G

Here is the TAB notation and chord diagram symbol for the D7 chord:

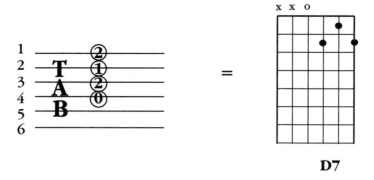

D7

The tablature examples shown thus far have indicated which frets are to be pressed by the left-hand fingers but haven't indicated which right-hand fingers to use. When TAB is also used to specify the right-hand fingers, you will see either the letters T, I, M, and R—which stand for the thumb, index, middle, and ring fingers—or P, I, M, and A—which stand for the same thing in Spanish: *pulgar, indice, medio,* and *annular*. Those letters appear directly beneath the TAB lines. For example, a thumb bass and pluck strum on a G chord could be shown this way in TAB:

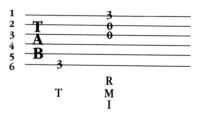

A fingerpicking strum for a G chord might be shown as follows:

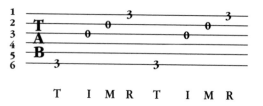

You would strike the third fret of the sixth string with your thumb, followed by the open third string with your first (I) finger, the open string with your second (M) finger, and then the third fret of the first string with your third (R) finger.

The timing of the notes and chords is not normally designated in TAB but left to the discretion of the performer, just as in reading chord symbols from a lead sheet you would play the chords in a tempo that would make sense in relation to what you were playing. However, in modern TAB there are cases of stems showing note values, but that is rare.

Before turning to the lead sheet of "Auld Lang Syne," finger a G chord with your left hand and follow the TAB directions for the right-hand fingerpicking strum. Begin with the thumb bass stroke with which you are familiar, followed by the individual plucking of the strings in the order specified. After you have done that several times, turn to the lead sheet of "Auld Lang Syne" and play simple thumb strums at first. After you have done that, follow the fingerpicking directions as they appear beneath the lead sheet. Don't be discouraged if you find the change from G to G7 in the third measure difficult to make. It will become easy within a surprisingly short time. Trust me!

−7−
More Songs and Strums

Now that you have played "Auld Lang Syne" in the key of G, try playing it in the key of A. Since A is the next higher letter, play an A chord
where the G chord is indicated, an E7 instead of a D7, a D instead of
C, and an A7 instead of G7. Use a simple thumb strum because the
fingerpicking directions in tablature apply only to the key of G.

Changing these chords in this way is called *transposing*. If you
had been using a capo, you could have used the same chord positions
you used for the key of G and the pitch would have been automati-
cally raised. (To get to the A pitch using the G chord positions, you
would put the capo on the *second* fret, not the first. That's because
the sequence of notes from G to A is G, G♯, A, *not* G directly to A.)
You also could use the G chord position in changing to the key of A
by using a fingered bar on the second fret. However, with a fingered
bar most of the chords would be very difficult to produce.

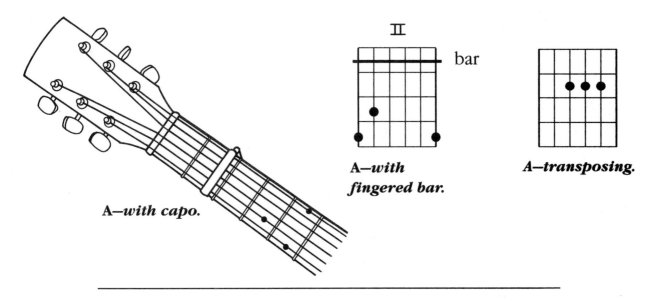

II

bar

A—*with
fingered bar.*

A—*transposing.*

A—*with capo.*

59

A much easier fingered bar position for an A chord is the E chord position with the bar on the fifth fret:

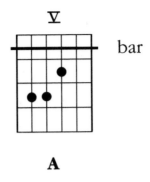

But this means learning different chord positions and not relying on just one way to form an A chord.

Obviously, if you always use a capo to change chords you won't have to learn this bar position. Just learn one chord form and let the capo change the pitch. And since a great many songs are based upon the same five or six different chords, a capo can have its advantages. However, if you take the time to learn the basics of note reading and chord relationships (see Appendix), you will have greater flexibility in playing and be able to produce many more beautiful harmonies.

THE CLAWHAMMER STRUM

There are many different styles of the so-called *clawhammer* finger-picking strum, which involves plucking *two* strings simultaneously on the first beat with the thumb and first finger and then alternating the pluck with the first finger and thumb. For example, finger the following C chord with your left hand:

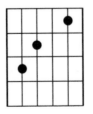

And in C, or 4/4 time (four beats to a measure), pluck as follows:

One Measure

Count (4/4 time)		1	2	3	4
String to Pluck	Thumb	5	–	3	–
	First finger	1	2	–	2

(Because you may see strums diagrammed this way as well as in tablature, I will provide examples in this form from time to time.)

As the diagram indicates, on the first beat of each measure you pluck the fifth string with your thumb and the first string with your first finger; on the second beat you pluck just the second string with your first finger; on the third beat you pluck the third string with your thumb; and on the fourth beat you pluck the second string with your first finger. Pluck the strings very slowly on the beats and in the order specified, noting the special accent you will be getting on each first beat because of the double pluck.

After you have successfully "clawed" the C chord, try the A chord. The same pattern that you applied to those chords can be used for the forms of the Am, A7, B7, and C7 chords diagrammed on page 54.

When forming chords with a left-hand finger on the sixth string, such as the G and G7 chords, you can begin with a thumb pluck on the sixth string instead of the fifth. That also applies to chords involving the sixth string, such as the Em and E7 chords, also diagrammed on page 54. For these chords the clawhammer diagram would be as follows:

One Measure

Count (4/4 time)		1	2	3	4
String to Pluck	Thumb	6	–	3	–
	First finger	1	2	–	2

Try this pattern using the E7 chord position. After doing that several times, claw the A chord pattern for four measures and then the E7 chord pattern for four measures. When you can do this relatively comfortably, play "Skip to My Lou" slowly, using the appropriate clawhammer strums for the A and E7 chords.

Starting note for singing: C# (second fret on second string).

Skip to My Lou

Flies in the but- ter- milk shoo fly shoo, Flies in the but- ter- milk

shoo fly shoo, Flies in the but- ter- milk shoo fly shoo, skip to my Lou my dar - ling.

*(Instead of Clawhammer, effective ending is two simple, emphatic thumb strums).

Note that the footnote to the last A chord indicates strumming the entire chord twice instead of fingerpicking the last word. Often the last chord in a song may be emphasized by a sudden *dampening* of the strings. This is done by covering the strings with the palm of your right hand immediately after the last strum. When ending songs played in any fingerpicking style, it is the usual practice to end on a fully strummed chord. In the case of a very soft, slow song it may be effective if you were to pluck one particular string lightly, allowing the final sound to fade.

A very popular variation of the clawhammer is to alternate the plucking of the strings. In learning this variation it is best to count the beats "one and, two and" rather than "one, two," as in the first clawhammer diagram. Try this alternating style using an A chord:

One Measure

Count (4/4 time)		1	and	2	and	3	and	4	and
String to Pluck {	Thumb	5		3		4		3	
	First finger	1	2	—	2	—	2	—	2

This pattern applies to any chord forms that do not involve the sixth string, such as the A or C chords. In the case of the E7 chord, in which you do pluck the sixth string, the pattern would be the same except that on each first beat a 6 would be indicated for the thumb instead of a 5. Otherwise, the remaining string and finger directions apply.

Now try the A chord for four measures followed by the E7 chord for four measures in the alternating style. Then try the C chord followed by the G7 chord in the same way.

There are times when it might sound better to begin this variation with your thumb on the fourth string rather than the fifth or sixth. This is certainly true in the case of chords that involve only the first four strings. For example, the 4–3 thumb pattern would apply to the Ddim7, Fm7, and Bm chords. In the case of the D and D7 chords you might prefer the 4–3 pattern even though the note A produced by the open fifth string is one of the notes in both chords. Here is a diagram of the 4–3 pattern:

One Measure

Count (4/4 time)		1	and	2	and	3	and	4	and
String to Pluck	Thumb	4		3		4		3	
	First finger	1	2	–	2	–	2	–	2

Since you will be fingerpicking the D7 chord in the next song, "I've Been Working on the Railroad," try it in accordance with the above fingerpicking pattern. After you have done that to your satisfaction, try playing the last two measures as follows: on the word "Dinah" do just the first two beats on the G chord and then do the next two beats on the D7 chord. In other words, the 4–3 fingerpicking pattern will remain the same, except that you won't begin with a claw when you change from G to D7. Also, just do the first two beats of the G chord in the last measure, substituting a final G chord thumb strum for the third and fourth beats. That's a better way to end the song.

I've Been Working on the Railroad

Starting note for singing: G (third string, open).

Moderately

Count: 1 and 2 and 3 and 4 and etc.

I've been work-ing on the rail-road all the live-long day. I've been work-ing on the rail-road to pass the time a-way. Can't you hear the whis-tle blow-ing? Rise up so ear-ly in the morn. Can't you hear the cap-tain shout-ing "Di-nah Blow Your Horn!"

—8—
Strumming in Duple and Triple Time

You now have learned six different strums: the thumb strum, the thumb bass and brush, the thumb bass and pluck, the thumb bass and fingerpick, the basic clawhammer, and the alternating clawhammer. Before going any further, try playing "I've Been Working on the Railroad" using all six strums—one at a time as well as mixing them up. Let your feelings be your guide in deciding when to change from one strum to another. You have already done so to a limited extent when you have changed from a fingerpicking strum to an emphatic thumb strum on a chord in the last measure of a song.

One good reason for using all six strums in "I've Been Working on the Railroad" is that you will become more aware of the differences among them. For example, when you use the simple thumb strum in the key of G, which is the key of the lead sheet, it won't matter much whether your thumb begins on the fifth or fourth string when you play the D7 chord. However, when you use the thumb bass and clawhammer strums, you will probably find it preferable to begin with your thumb on the fourth string on the D7 chord even though the fifth open string is harmonically part of that chord. I say "probably" because in terms of popular music nothing is carved in granite. If you were playing a Villa-Lobos piece or almost any classical music, you would have to play the notes exactly as written by the composer. Unless you play the "Moonlight Sonata" exactly as Beethoven wrote it, it won't be the "Moonlight Sonata." However, there is no *one* particular way to play "By the Time I Get to Phoenix," "Johnny B. Goode,"

"Love Me Tender," "You Light Up My Life," or "Moon River" for those songs to be perfectly valid musical renditions.*

So far you have played songs in the keys of C, G, and A. This is the time for you not only to try the different strums you have learned but also to try playing the songs in different keys. For example, in a song that required the use of only two chords, one was the basic, or home-plate, chord and the other the chord of tension, the seventh chord. In the key of C you used the C chord and the G7, G being the fifth letter after C. In the key of G the seventh chord would be D7, D being the fifth letter after G (remember—the only letters used are A through G). And in the key of A the seventh chord would be E7.

In songs where you use three different chords, a similar sequential relationship usually occurs. In the key of C, for example, the F chord is almost always the third most important chord; in the key of G, it's the C chord; and in A, it's the D chord. In other words, the third chord is usually *fourth* in the alphabetical sequence. These three chords are referred to as the *tonic, subdominant,* and *dominant seventh*—the one, four, and five chords. So in the key of C the sequence is the C, F, and G7 chords; in G it's the G, C, and D7 chords; in A it's the A, D, and E7 chords.

It should now be apparent that in the key of C the C chord is the *one* (tonic) chord, whereas in the key of G it becomes the *four* (subdominant) chord. What is the significance of this? Once you establish a certain chord as being home plate—the chord that your ear accepts as the chord of resolution—its relationship to the other chords is different from when those *other* chords become home plate to your ear.

If all this information about chord relationships seems somewhat complicated now, don't worry. You will still be able to fully understand everything that follows.

So far, of the six songs you have played in the order in which they appeared, all except "Clementine" have been in duple time. Instead of four beats to a measure, "Clementine" has only three. Because you were just learning the C and G7 chords, I thought it simpler to indicate thumb strums on each first beat only, allowing you more time to

*All of these songs can be played using only the basic common chords diagrammed in this book.

change chords. I could have indicated the strumming on *each* of the three beats as follows:

Beats:	1	2	3		1	2	3
Chord:	C	C	C		C	C	C
	In a cav	−	ern,	in a	can −	yon,	ex−ca−

Beats:	1	2	3		1	2	3
Chord:	C	C	C		G7	G7	G7
	va	− ting	for a		mine,	——	lived a . . .

Adapting the strums you have learned to triple time poses no problem. Using the simple thumb strum, you simply strum on just the first beat or on all three as above—or perhaps on just the second or third beats in cases where a special effect is called for, such as in certain Latin rhythms. When you use the thumb bass and brush or the thumb bass and pluck, you simply strum once with your thumb and brush or pluck twice for the next two beats.

Often a piano part is written in a key that is not easy for most amateur guitarists. In such cases, an additional set of chords may appear above those that are in the key of the piano part but which are in an easier key for the guitar. For example, on the sheet music for "She Believes in Me," by Steve Gibb, one of Kenny Rogers's greatest hits, the piano part is in the key of B♭, not the easiest key for guitar. So above the B♭ chords are chords for the key of G, a much easier key. In addition, there's a note at the beginning of the song that specifies placing a capo on the third fret so that the G chord positions will have the sound of the B♭ chords. (The capo on the first fret would raise the pitch from G to G♯; on the second fret, to A; and on the third fret, to B♭). If you were accompanying someone who was playing a piano part written in B♭, using the capo would result in your being in tune with the piano—that is, in the same key. However, if you just played the G chord positions without a capo, the song would sound well in the key of G, but then the pianist would have to do the transposing to be in tune with you. If you took the time to learn the B♭ chords, all of the options would be open to you.

I wrote the following lead sheet for "Clementine" (see page 69) in the key of F to provide a tuneful opportunity for you to learn the F and C7 chords. Also, I've indicated the G and D7 chords above the F chord positions so that you can play "Clementine" in G as well as in F. Since you first played "Clementine" in C and then in A, you now will be able to play it in four different keys! But remember to sing or hum on the correct starting note, which in this case is the same as the note of the key in which you are playing.

On the diagrams for the F and C7 chords, I've purposely indicated a *full* bar for the F chord although it can be formed by using a *half* bar—that is, by just covering the first two, three, or four strings with your first left-hand finger. There are two reasons why a full bar is better: first, it is one of the basic bar positions that can be moved up the frets to produce different major chords—F to F♯ to G, etc.—so that you can play many, if not all, of the simple major chords; and second, the full bar permits you to include the sixth string in your strums. With the half bar the fifth or sixth strings would not be part of the F chord.

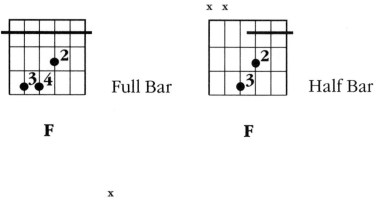

Full Bar   Half Bar

F   F

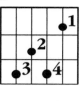

C7

Now try playing "Clementine" in 3/4 time (as indicated in the time signature) with the thumb bass and brush and thumb bass and pluck strums.

Clementine

Starting note for singing: in F-F (third fret on fourth string);
in G-G (third string, open).

The best way to illustrate the fingerpicking strums in 3/4, or triple, time is to use tablature. Instead of writing out the complete song, I will simply do the first three measures of the G chord and one measure of the D7 chord. After you have done the fingerpicking in G, you should do it using the F and C7 chords. You should begin in G since the G and D7 chords are easier to form. Before you strum the song from the lead sheet, fingerpick the G and D7 chords from the following tablature measures:

Clementine

Again, after fingerpicking in G, do it in F using the bar chord F and C7 positions as diagrammed on page 68.

As for the clawhammer fingerpicking styles, here are three examples in tablature, again using the G chord:

At this point you might try devising your own clawhammer styles that seem most suitable for the particular song you are playing as well as the chords involved.

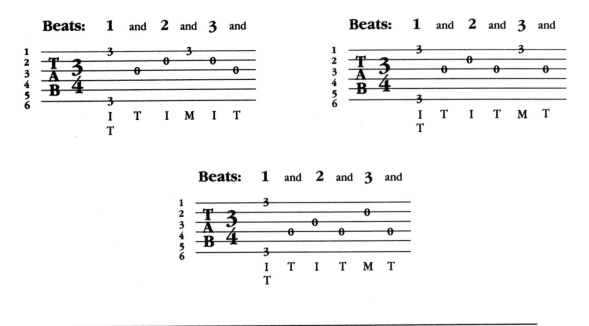

—9—
Signs and Symbols, Pick Strums, Boogie-Woogie, and the Blues

In this lesson I am delighted to be able to use the lead sheet of "To All the Girls I've Loved Before." The song originally became popular when it was recorded by Willie Nelson and Julio Iglesias, two singers who follow different musical paths. Nelson is a confirmed country singer, and Iglesias is famous for his renditions of the great standard romantic ballads as well as current pop, Latin, and jazz tunes. The fact that two such diverse musical personalities could have collaborated so successfully indicates an important fact about the song: the intrinsic versatility of its combination of words and music allows it to be performed in any of the popular genres—country, pop, jazz, romantic ballad, etc. In the language of the music business, this is what is known as a *crossover* song.

But that's not all. The song is written in the key of G—ideal for guitarists—and can be played using only the basic tonic, subdominant, and dominant seventh chords (G, C, and D7), even though others are indicated. (Often lead sheets specify chords that do not necessarily have to be played, something very important for you to know when you read from sheet music or fake books—more about this later.)

Also, the song provides you an opportunity to become familiar with the various signs and symbols found in lead sheets and is an ideal vehicle for learning how to use a pick, play a melody, and develop the technique of hammering on and pulling off.

To All the Girls I've Loved Before

Lyrics by Hal David
Music by Albert Hammond

Moderately Slow, expressively ♩ = 84

To all the girls I've loved be - fore, who trav - eled in and
once ca - ressed, and may I say I've
shared my life, who now are some one

out my door; I'm glad they came a - long, I ded - i - cate this
held the best; for help - ing me to grow, I owe a lot, I
els - e's wife; I'm glad they came a - long, I ded - i - cate this

To Coda

song to all the girls I've loved be - fore, To all the girls I've
know, to all the girls I've loved be - fore,
song to all the girls I've

2.

The winds of change are al - ways blow - ing and ev - 'ry time I tried to

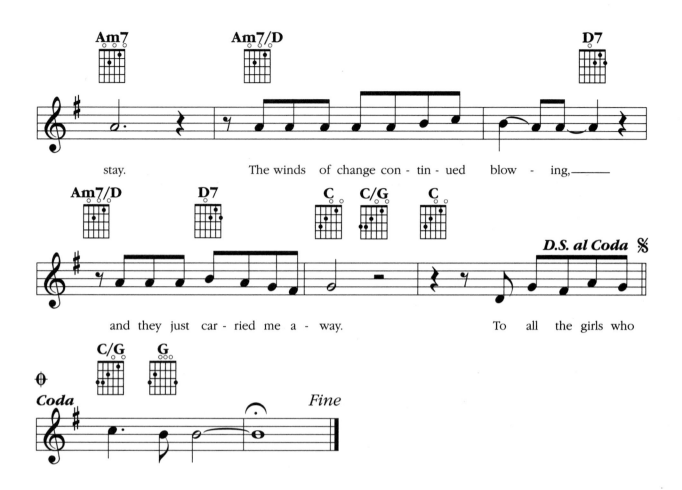

stay.   The winds of change con - tin - ued   blow - ing,———

and they just car - ried me a - way.   To   all   the girls who

Coda   *Fine*

SIGNS AND SYMBOLS

The two dots and the double bar before the word "loved" at the beginning of the song is a repeat sign:

In songs where the melody remains the same although the words
change, it is common practice to use repeat signs at appropriate places
so the notes of the melody don't have to be rewritten. This song begins with a pickup, so the first full measure is the one beginning with

the word "loved." Above the eighth measure, then, is where you see the *first ending* sign:

> 1.

The repeat sign at the end of that measure means that you should go back to the first repeat sign and continue with the second line of lyrics. When you get to the first ending the second time around, skip it and continue with the *second ending*:

> 2.

Proceed until you get to the measure above which you see "*D.S. al Coda* 𝄋." The *D.S.* stands for the Italian words *dal segno* ("from the sign"), meaning go from this S-shaped sign, 𝄋, back to the one above the first measure and continue with the third set of lyrics. The "*al Coda*" means that when you get to the coda sign 𝄌 at the end of the sixth measure, play from the coda sign at the last two measures. *Fine*, of course, means "the end" in Italian, the language used most frequently in describing various musical signs, symbols, and directions.

Repeat signs often can be confusing, and sometimes you may have to use common sense to figure out when to go back to what, but for the most part they are relatively easy to understand.

There are times when there will be no repeat sign or segno (𝄋) at the beginning of a song and you will come to the words "*Da Capo*" at the end. That means go back to the beginning—"take it from the top." You may see the words *al fine*, meaning "to the end," as in "*D.C. al fine*" or "*D.S. al fine*." In the first case, where *D.C.* stands for *Da Capo*, you are to go back to the beginning and end when you come to the word *fine*. In the case of *D.S. al fine*, where D.S. stands for *dal segno*, you are to go back to the S-shaped sign and continue until you reach *fine*.

The directions as to the speed, or tempo, of the song (♩ = 84) below the title mean that quarter notes are to be played at the rate of 84 beats per minute. Obviously, unless you have a metronome that you can set at that rate, you simply play the song at whatever tempo pleases you. As a matter of fact, you may choose to play the song freely—not metronomically—so that you can give expression to certain notes by giving them more or less time.

Chord diagrams are another important specification on lead sheets, and the Am7 diagrams need some explanation. The first Am7 diagram is followed by Am7/D, yet both diagrams are exactly the same. The reason for this has to do with the fact that many pianists ignore the piano parts found in sheet music and use the guitar chord symbols as a guide to which notes to play when accompanying the melody. The D after the Am7 symbol is a suggestion that a pianist use the note D as the bass note over which to play the notes of an Am7 chord. Actually, that makes the chord a D suspended seventh plus 9, which could be symbolized as follows:

x

D7sus+9

This chord is so easy to play that I suggest you substitute it for the Am7/D. (Later I will explain the effect of using suspended chords and how the tension they create is resolved.)

Generally, a slash sign in guitar chord symbols means that the note after the slash should be considered as the bass note. I say "considered" because it is not always possible to achieve it literally in certain cases where it would require an impossible stretching of the fingers. However, in the case of the C/G symbol, above the measure before the first ending, the G is easy to add to the C chord by pressing the third fret of the sixth string. You can use your third finger to press both the third frets of the fifth and sixth strings:

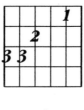

C/G

Incidentally, you can simplify matters by omitting the above C/G chord and simply continuing to strum the G chord. This is another example of how to use chord symbols as guides rather than as musts.

I suggest that you familiarize yourself with "To All the Girls I've Loved Before" by using a simple thumb strum, four beats to a measure. Then follow that with a simple thumb bass and brush strum, allowing one beat for the bass and one for the brush. A four-beat measure would then consist of bass, brush, bass, brush. You might try alternating the bass notes from time to time. (You may prefer to stay on the same bass note when playing certain chords.)

Next, try a favorite country strum of mine, what I call the country shuffle brush strum. Begin by fingering a G chord and brush all the strings in a downward motion with the first, second, and third fingers of your right hand. It is similar to the simple thumb strum except that you are now using three fingers instead of one.

Now, in order to achieve the "country" effect, do an emphatic downstroke followed by a quick down-and-up stroke—in a "boom-chicka-boom" rhythm. In tablature the strum can be illustrated as follows (arrows indicate whether the strum is up or down):

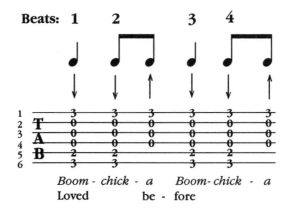

Note that I didn't include all the strings on the upstrokes because it isn't necessary most of the time to brush all the notes on upstrokes. It may not be necessary to brush all the strings on the downstrokes either. For example, using the D7 chord specified for this song, upstrokes *and* downstrokes will sound best if you strum only the first four strings.

This strum also works well with "I've Been Working on the Railroad," particularly since it includes the A7 and B7 chords as well as the G, C, and D7 chords.

PICK STRUMS

Picks come in various shapes and sizes and can be made of different materials—tortoise shell, for example—although most are made of plastic. Some picks are thicker and less flexible than others, and your choice will depend upon the kind of music you wish to play, what gauge of strings you are using, and, above all, how it feels when you strum with it.

Hold the pick between your thumb and first finger just tightly enough so that it doesn't fall out of your fingers when you strum with it. Hold it so that the most pointed corner is the one that will strike the strings in the same perpendicular direction that you used when you did the simple thumb strum. Since the pick is much thinner and firmer than the soft flesh of the thumb, it will produce a more brilliant and somewhat sharper sound.

Obviously, you can't do a thumb bass and pluck strum with a pick, nor can it duplicate any of the various fingerpicking styles. However, because of the pungency it adds to the sounds it produces, you may prefer it when playing certain songs. Play "To All the Girls I've Loved Before" beginning with a simple strum analogous to the first thumb strum you learned. Follow that with a bass and brush strum. To play the G chord, for example, you would pick the sixth string, coming to rest on the fifth before brushing the rest of the strings.

Another favorite country strum using a pick—a strum that Garth Brooks uses—is what I call a country double shuffle strum. Instead of the "boom-chicka-boom-chicka" strum you did with your fingers, you double the shuffle with your pick by strumming a "boom-chicka-*chicka*-chicka" rhythm. As in the case of finger strumming, you don't have to strike all six strings on the up strums. For example, finger the G chord position you have been using and strum with a pick as follows:

One 4/4 Measure

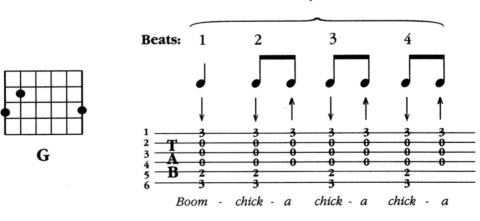

This strum is effective for hundreds of country favorites, such as "Through the Years," "You Needed Me," "Heartbreak Hotel," "Crazy," and "Hey, Good Lookin'!" It is also easily adaptable to country songs in 3/4 time, such as "Are You Lonesome Tonight?" "Could I Have This Dance?" and "Mexicali Rose" as well as romantic ballads that run the gamut from "Always" to "Answer me," "Try to Remember," "Tenderly," and "Moon River." For songs in triple time, the strumming pattern would simply be "boom-chicka-chicka, boom-chicka-chicka." Using the G chord again, this is how it would look:

One 3/4 Measure

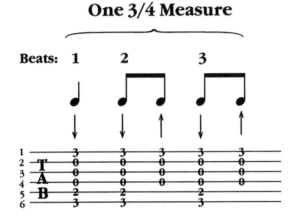

"Clementine" is a song in triple time that you have already strummed in the key of G using only the G and D7 chords. I suggest that you try it using this strum with a pick and get the feeling of doing partial strums on the *up*strokes. You might even find it musically appropriate to do a partial *down* strum on the second and third beats as well. Partial strumming with fingers or a pick enables you to feel more relaxed while you're playing.

Finally, with regard to strumming with a pick, you can copy some of the patterns you used when doing the fingerpicking strums. For example, the thumb bass and brush strum can be done by clearly picking the bass note of a chord followed by a downstroke of the remaining strings. Also, instead of one downward brush you can add an up strum.

On "Clementine," in 3/4 time, the strum can be picked as follows:

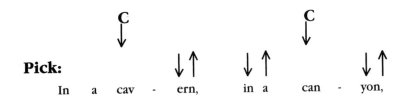

Down-up strums are generally done in a "oomp-a, oomp-a, oomp-a, oomp-a" shuffle rhythm, with the "oomp"'s slightly longer than the "a"'s. A simple shuffle strum may be illustrated as follows:

One Measure

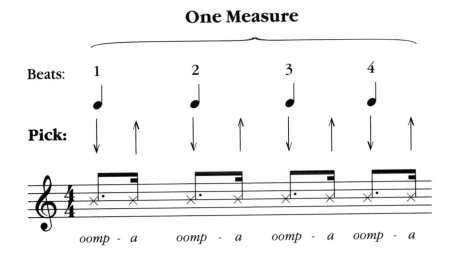

Partial strumming can be applied to this shuffle strum, particularly when used to accompany popular romantic ballads such as "Close to You," "All the Way," "The Way We Were," and "Unforgettable."

Whether you wish to play the great jazz standards of the Big Band era or folk, country, blues, or even rock 'n' roll, you now know all the basic strums in order to get started. You should know enough to play those songs from the vocal lines in sheet music or from the lead sheets in fake books. You might need to refer to the diagrams of popular guitar chords in the Appendix, but that effort would be minuscule compared to the satisfaction you will derive from playing your favorite songs.

THE BLUES

The best way to wrap up this lesson is by discussing the blues. In terms of harmonic structure, blues music was the forerunner of all the jazz and popular music (as opposed to classical) that followed, whether ragtime, swing, country, or rock. The major difference between the blues and the other styles is that it is based on a group of twelve measures rather than eight, sixteen, or thirty-two. The twelve measures involve the one, four, and five chords referred to on page 66—namely, the tonic, subdominant, and dominant chords. Here is a "typical" twelve-bar blues pattern as it would be strummed in the key of G. The slash marks represent the four beats in each measure on which the designated chord can be strummed:

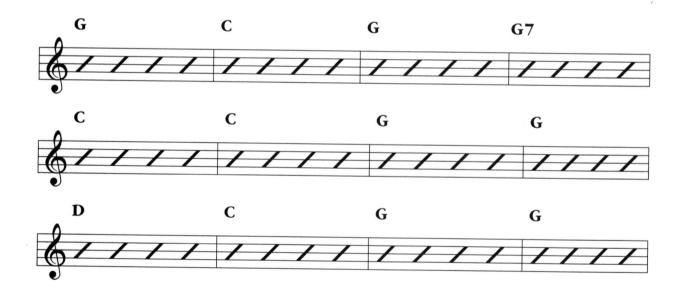

Often the last measure is divided between the G and D7 chords when the sequence starts over again. The D7 chord creates the feeling of wanting to come back to the beginning. In that case the last measure would be shown as follows:

Or, instead of the G preceding the D7 chord in the last measure, you might substitute an Am7:

Innumerable variations of the blues have been developed through the years. The very early blues patterns, which originated shortly before the turn of the century and were popularized by W. C. Handy just before World War I, were structured like this:

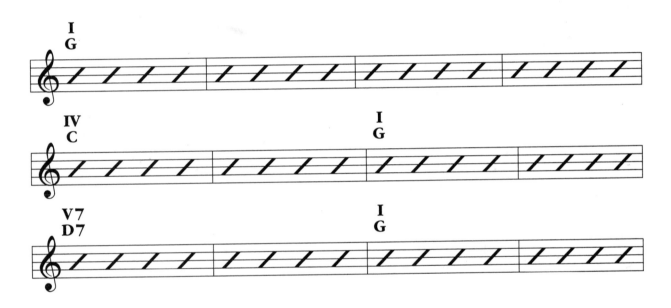

Chuck Berry has used this pattern in many of his songs, including "Johnny B. Goode," a song he wrote in the 1950s and still one of the most popular *rock* songs of all time.

The blues pattern that I called "typical" is one of the most widely used forms when playing boogie-woogie. It is in the key of A on the next page; an effective key for the guitar because the chord changes are relatively easy to make. (Use the *alternate* version of the E7 chord shown on page 54 because it will sound better than its counterpart.)

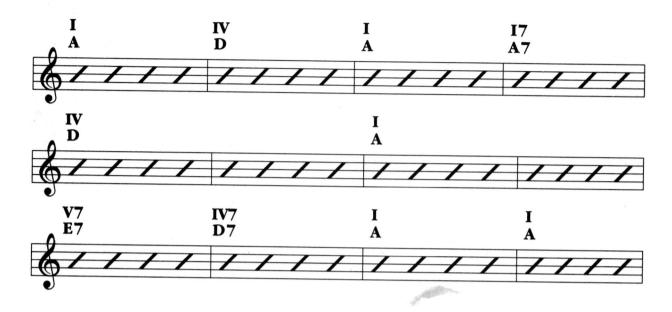

You can split the last measure between the A and E7 chords, as you did with the G and D7 chords in the key of G.

I added the Roman numerals I, IV, and V above the one, four, and five chords (tonic, subdominant, and dominant) so that you will be able to play the blues in any other key. For example, in the key of D, the I stands for D, the IV stands for G, and the V stands for A. Before going to the next lesson, try the blues in the keys of D, C, and E using this same pattern:

Key	Pattern		Key	Pattern
D	D–G–D–D7		C	C–F–C–C7
	G–G–D–D			F–F–C–C
	A7–G7–D–D			G7–F7–C–C

Key	Pattern
E	E–A–E–E7
	A–A–E–E
	B7–A7–E–E

−10−
Left-Hand Techniques, Melodies, and Popular Chord Progressions

Now is the time and place to take a giant step in your progress by learning some of the more advanced techniques involving your left hand. *Hammering on* and *pulling off* are two easy ways to put your left-hand fingers into play, so to speak.

HAMMERING ON

You can produce a tone on a string by "hammering" on it with one of your left-hand fingers while it is vibrating. For example, finger a C chord with your left hand. Before strumming, lift your finger off the fifth string and pluck that string with your right-hand thumb as though you were going to start a thumb bass and brush strum. While the open fifth string is sounding, "hammer" your third finger down on the third fret of the open fifth string, thereby producing a different note. (The open fifth string produces the note A, and the hammering of its third fret produces the higher note C.) After the hammer stroke, continue brushing the remaining strings with your thumb—in other words, do a thumb bass and brush strum. The hammering-on trick thus enables you to produce two different notes with only one strum—in this case, the initial thumb bass part.

In tablature, the hammering of the third fret of the open fifth string (producing the sound of the open A followed by the C above it) may be illustrated in one of these ways:

The slur indicates that only *one* strum (with a pick or finger) should be used to produce those notes. The H means that the second note should be produced by hammering the third fret of the fifth string, which has been strummed while it was open.

Do this C chord hammering on a few times until you begin to get the feel of it. After a while you will discover that you don't have to hammer too hard to produce the second tone. Merely pressing your finger on the fret firmly will be enough to result in a pleasing tone. Actually, if this technique were not already known as hammering on, I would call it *pressing on*.

Now, instead of brushing only once after hammering on, brush twice—hammer (thumb bass), brush, brush, hammer (thumb bass), brush, brush, etc.—to the count of "one, two, three, one, two three." The first beat should be on the hammer, not the strum. It is important to remember that even though two notes are produced they only take up a *single* beat in a 3/4 *or* 4/4 rhythm pattern. The hammered note is normally the one that occurs on the beat, and the preceding one fits in almost as though the two notes were played together.

Hammering on doesn't have to be done on an open string. It can be used on strings where a fret is already pressed, and the second note can be hammered on any fret as high as you can reach while holding the first note in place. For example, press the first finger of your left hand on the fourth fret of the fourth string. Strum that string, and while it produces a sound keep your first finger in place and hammer the next higher (fifth) fret of that string with your second finger. Or press your first left-hand finger on the first fret of the first string, strum it, and hammer the third fret of that string with your third finger. Here's another example:

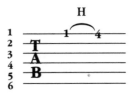

After strumming first string with first finger on first fret, hammer fourth fret with fourth (pinky) finger, keeping first finger firmly pressed on first fret.

"Clementine," a three-beat song that involves the C and G7 chords, is a good song for you to start using the hammering-on technique. Here, in tablature, is how a measure of the C chord and one of the G7 chord might be illustrated:

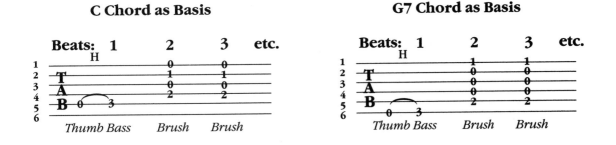

The hammer-brush-brush pattern can be done with your thumb or a pick; it would be good practice for you to play it both ways, beginning with your thumb. Above the lyrics I have indicated when to hammer and brush and when to change chords from one to the other.

Clementine

Starting note: C (fourth fret of fifth string)
Hammer and brush only on the word, syllable, or dash indicated.

H   B   B   H   B   B   HB   B   H   B   B
C   G7
In a cav—ern, in a can—yon, ex—ca—va—ting for a mine,—lived a

H   B   B   H   B   B   H   B   B   H   B   B
C   G7   C
min—er, for—ty nin—er, and his daugh—ter, Clem—en—tine.—Oh, my

H   B   B   H   B   B   HB   B   H   B   B
                                            G7
dar—ling, oh, my dar—ling, oh, my dar—ling, Clem—en—tine,—you are

H   B   B   H   B   B   H   B   B   H   B
C   G7   C*
lost and gone for—ev—er, dread—ful sor—ry, Clem—en—tine.—

*Strum last full chord emphatically; then dampen strings immediately with palm of right hand for effect.

Instead of a brush on the second and third beats, you can try plucking the first three strings on those beats. After that you can follow the hammering on with the fingerpicking pattern you learned on page 70. Although that example showed the pattern using the G and D7 chords, you can adapt it to the C and G7 chords. However, if you try the hammer-fingerpick strum in the key of G, using the G and D7 chords, do the hammering on the open sixth string: strum the open string and hammer the third fret for the G chord. For the D7 chord, the hammered string would be the third, leaving it open to begin with and hammering the second fret with your second finger. The fingerpicking could then be done by repeating the hammered note with your first right-hand finger, followed by the second and first strings as before. In tablature that could be illustrated this way:

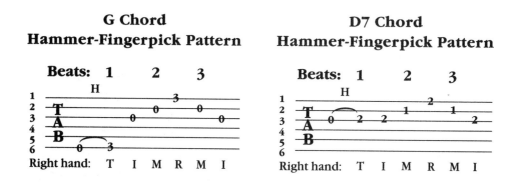

G Chord
Hammer-Fingerpick Pattern

D7 Chord
Hammer-Fingerpick Pattern

Or instead of repeating the hammered note, you can do an alternating fingerpick:

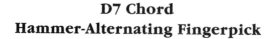

D7 Chord
Hammer-Alternating Fingerpick

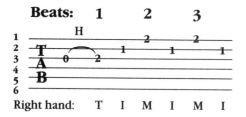

Hammering on also may be used to produce *three* tones: simply remove the finger that did the hammering so that the vibrating string will sound the initial note again. To do this, place the first finger of your left hand on the second fret of the sixth string. Strum that string

---

and hammer the third fret with the second finger of your left hand. While the string is still sounding, remove your second finger and the sound will revert to that of the second-fretted sixth string. Here it is in tablature:

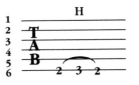

The slur over all three notes indicates that they should be produced by one strum.

This technique is particularly useful when playing melodies. It is most effective when done quickly; otherwise, you might as well strum the individual notes.

PULLING OFF

This brings us to the subject of pulling off, which, as the name implies, means producing a note by pulling one of your left-hand fingers off a string. For example, place your first finger on the third fret of the first string and your third finger on the fifth fret. While keeping both fingers in position, pluck the first string, thereby producing the sound of the fifth fret; then pull your third finger off the fifth fret to produce the sound of the third fret. This is usually diagrammed as follows:

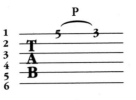

In chord-diagram form it may be shown this way:

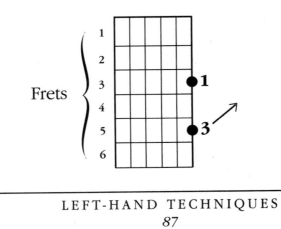

As with hammering on, pulling off can be used to produce more than two notes. For example, press the first three frets of the second string with your first, second, and third fingers:

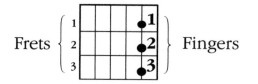

While holding this position, pluck the second string and pull off your fingers, one at a time, beginning with your third finger. The last note will be the open B string produced by pulling off your first finger.

You can end this downward sequence by strumming a G chord, giving you an easy musical phrase that can be used to end songs in the key of G, such as "I've Been Working on the Railroad" (page 64) and "To All the Girls I've Loved Before" (page 72). If you feel you need an extra beat at the end, you can strum the G chord again, emphatically, and then dampen it with the palm of your right hand, or you can simply pluck the first string, which will produce a G (since you have already pressed the third fret for the G chord position).

You also can use this phrase as an intro by following the G chord with a D7 chord. Try it with the two songs I mentioned in the last paragraph.

PLAYING MELODIES

The eight-note opening melody "To All the Girls I've Loved Before" can be played several ways using the hammering and pulling techniques. Here is the tablature for the simplest version, which involves only one pull off:

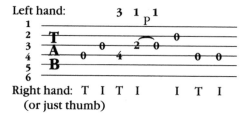

The reason I provided the alternate fingering of thumb and index finger is that alternating the fingers gives you greater agility in playing melodies—something you will gain as you become more advanced.

Another way is to begin with a hammer on the fourth open string with your third finger:

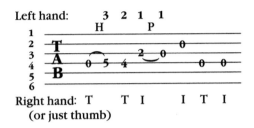

These two variations of the beginning of "To All the Girls" are a good introduction to playing melodies as well as a more interesting way to work on the techniques of hammering on and pulling off. The same can be said for the so-called G run, a series of notes you will hear quite frequently in country music, especially bluegrass, although it is easily adaptable to many styles of music. It is used to end songs, to end phrases within songs, and to accent certain parts of songs. It is called the G run because that's the key in which it occurs most often; however, it is playable in other keys frequently used by guitarists.

Here is one of the most popular variations of the G run as it would appear in sheet music and in tablature:

The G Run

(Brush — entire G chord, if you wish)

The notations in treble clef are there in case you can read music or want to learn. Also, if you happen to have a keyboard or any other instrument that can play those notes, you will be able to get the sound of the G run before attempting it on the guitar. However, that is not necessary because you now can read tablature, and I've tried to make the example clearer by indicating the fingering for your right and left hands.

Your right hand simply uses your thumb to do the strumming—three times in the first measure and twice in the last. Incidentally, your thumb on only three strums in the first measure will result in producing *seven* different tones! That shows some of the advantages of hammering on and pulling off in playing melodies.

Fingering for the left hand is not normally shown in tablature, but I thought it would be helpful for anyone with a minimum amount of experience reading from it. By using your third finger to form the last chord, you will be positioned not only to brush the first four strings but to use your first and second fingers to form the entire G chord if you wish.

As I have already pointed out, the methodology of tablature is not uniform. In most cases you will find prefatory explanations of how to follow a particular version. But for the most part, common sense can almost always guide you in interpreting a given rendition because there may be only one way to do so. Here are two examples that do not specify whether hammering on or pulling off is called for. Yet in the first case you cannot produce the required notes without hammering on, and in the second case only pulling off will do the trick unless you choose to disregard the slurs and strum the notes individually or slide your fingers from note to note. However, a slide is usually designated by a straight line or a slur with an *s* above it.

CHORD PROGRESSIONS

Chord progressions are a series of different chords that lead to one another because they create a feeling of making musical sense—a feeling of inevitability. The simplest progression that has been previously explained is the dominant seventh (or *five* chord) leading to the tonic (the *one* chord). For example, the tension created by playing the G7 chord is resolved by playing the C chord. When you learned to strum "Clementine," you undoubtedly felt how the G7 chords led to the C chords whether or not you could read a note of music.

Going from the dominant seventh to the tonic, or V7 to I, is perhaps the most frequently used two-chord progression. I say "perhaps" because going from the four chord (not as a seventh) to the one (subdominant to tonic, or IV-I) is used as the "Amen" after many hymns and other forms of church music. That progression is called a *plagal cadence*; if you want to hear it, play an F chord and then a C chord. Or, if you establish G as the home-plate key, play a C chord (the IV chord in the succession of notes from G to C) followed by the G chord.

A popular three-chord progression is II-V-I. In the key of G this would mean Am7, the two chord, followed by the D7, the five chord, and ending with G, the one chord. (The reason why the two chord is a *minor* seventh is too technical to go into in this lesson; see the Appendix for an explanation.) You will find this progression at the end of the first stanza of "To All the Girls I've Loved Before" (page 72). In the key of D that progression would be Em7 to A7 to D. (Those chords are diagrammed on page 54.) When you play these three-chord progressions, give each chord two simple thumb strums just to get the feel of them.

In many popular songs the II-IV-I progression will begin with the two chord as a *dominant* seventh. Thus, in C it would be D7-G7-C; in G it would be A7-D7-G; in D it would be E7-A7-D. Try them all, playing the chords from memory (which by now you may very well be able to do) or by referring to page 54.

A very popular four-chord progression is VIm7-IIm7-V7-I. In the key of G the progression would be Em7-Am7-D7-G; it will sound best to you if you begin with the one chord, G, and give each chord two strums. You can also make dominant sevenths of the VI and II chords—E7-A7; try playing the progression both ways.

The first version of this four-chord progression (using the *minor* seventh for the VI and II chords) has been used as the harmonic basis for thousands of the most popular songs ever composed. When you find yourself reading chords from vocal lines in sheet music or fake books you will be amazed to see how many times you will run across this sequence of chords. As a matter of fact, if you ever wanted to write an original song or set a lyric to music, just keep strumming G-Em7-Am7-D7-G, etc., and you might come up with a hit! (I specified the key of G because the four chords in both versions—with minor sevenths and dominant sevenths—appear on page 54. For the modern jazz versions of these chords, including this progression in almost any key, see "Basic Jazz Chords" in the Appendix.)

Here is the I–VI–II–V progression in the most commonly used keys for guitar, using the modern jazz chords (see page 102) as the basis. The first letter represents the key of the progression.

I	VI	II	V
C	Am7	Dm7	G7
D	Bm7	Em7	A7
E	C♯m7	F♯m7	B7
F	Dm7	Gm7	C7
G	Em7	Am7	D7
A	F♯m7	Bm7	E7

Try playing these progressions, two strums to a chord, and ending on the one chord.

The best way I can think of to end this last lesson is to show you some really great modern jazz chord progressions that produce some of the most beautiful guitar sounds—to my ears, at least. But first, a few prefatory remarks:

In modern jazz three-note chords are seldom used. For example, instead of a simple C chord, where only the notes C, E, G are used, the modern jazz musician will play a major sixth—C, E, G, A (A being the sixth note in the scale of C)—or a major seventh—C, E, G, B (B being the seventh note in the scale, not B♭, which would make it a *dominant* seventh).

Also, many times chord substitutions sound very pleasant and may be easier to play than a particular designated chord. For example, in the first progression, basically a I–VI–II–V sequence, the last chord is a minor sixth instead of the usual dominant seventh. Instead of a D7 (the V chord in G, the key of the progression), I have indicated an Am6. The reason is that a D7 chord consists of a D, F♯, A, and C; the Am6, from the sixth string to the first, consists of A, F♯, C, E, and A again. (The fifth string is *muted*—see page 101 for an explanation of this term.) On the guitar, the way those notes are voiced—spread apart—allows them to sound like a D7, particularly after the preceding chords. That's why I put a D7 in parentheses below the diagram of the Am6 chord on page 98.

Finally, keep in mind that ninth, eleventh, and even thirteenth chords can be effectively replaced by simple dominant sevenths. The latter may not sound as rich but are fine enough for beginners and often just as musically satisfying.

In the following progressions, the number in parentheses above the chord refers to the diagram for that chord on page 102; the slash marks beneath the chords indicate the number of strums. I hope you try these chord progressions and derive as much satisfaction as I do when playing them—as intros, fill-ins, or endings.

---

(1)	(2)	(3)	(4)
GM7	**Em7**	**Am7**	**Am6**
//	//	//	//

etc., ending on GM7 or leading into a song

---

(1)	(2)	(3)	(4)	(5)
GM7	**Em7**	**Am7**	**Am6**	***D13♭5♭9**
//	//	//	/	/

etc., as above

---

(1)	(3)		(3)		(3)	(4)	(5)
GM7	**Bm7**	on 7th	**B♭m7**	on 6th	**Am7**	**Am6**	***D13♭5♭9**
//	/	instead of 5th fret	/	fret	//	/	/

etc., as above

---

(1)	(2)	(3)	(4)
GM7	***A13♭9**	**Am7**	**Am6**
//	//	//	//

etc., as above

---

(1)	(7)	(3)	(4)	(5)
GM7	***A13♭9**	**Am7**	**Am6**	***D13♭5♭9**
//	//	//	/	/

etc. as above

---

*See page 102.

These progressions can all be moved up the frets, one at a time, as far up the fingerboard as comfortable. By doing this you will train your fingers to mute strings where necessary and to achieve greater mobility.

I hope that through the lessons in this book I have given you a good start to a very happy ending—or should I say a new beginning?

Appendix

CHORD SYMBOLS

C or CM	=	C major
Cm	=	C minor
C7	=	C seventh (short for C *dominant* seventh)
CM7	=	C major seventh
Cm7	=	C minor seventh
C6	=	C sixth (short for C *major* sixth)
Cm6	=	C minor sixth
C7sus4 or C7sus	=	C suspended seventh
Cdim7 or C°7	=	C diminished seventh
C7♭5	=	C seventh flat the fifth
C/G	=	C major chord with G as the lowest (or *bass*) note. Notes that follow slashes after any of the above symbols mean the same thing: those notes are to be the *root*, or bottom, notes of the particular chord.

The same note may be called by two different names: C♯ or D♭, F♯ or G♭; B may be called C♭ just as E may be called F♭ or F may be called E♯. This is explained in greater detail later in this Appendix (see Music Notation), but its relevance with respect to this table is that where the diminished seventh chords are shown you will see C♯°7 and not D♭°7 or F♯°7 and not G♭°7. I simply chose the most commonly used designations with respect to guitar chords.

THE MOST COMMON POPULAR GUITAR CHORDS

Some of the following chords may have two different symbols. For example, in the Dominant Seventh Flat Five category you will see A7♭5 specified also as E♭7♭5; or in the case of the Diminished Seventh category there are three basic chords, each having four different symbols. The reason for this is simply that a four-note chord may be played four different ways: any one of the four notes may be used as the lowest, or bass, note of the chord. C, E, G, and B♭, the notes of the C7 chord, may be voiced as E, G, B♭, C or even out of order—G, C, B♭, E.

Often, the different voicings will not change the main effect of the chord, although the quality of the sound will be different. However, there are times when transposition of the same notes will not produce the sound of the expected chord. For example, all minor seventh chords have the same notes as major sixths: Em7 is made up of E, G, B, and D, while G6 is made up of G, B, D, and E—the same notes differently voiced. Nevertheless, in most cases on the guitar the sound of the minor seventh will prevail unless the key note of the major sixth chord is played as the bass note. Thus, B, D, E, G or D, G, B, E will sound more like an Em7 than a G6.

In the case of minor sixth chords, although they do not have the very same notes as the sevenths and ninths of the same key note, they are often fine substitutes and sometimes may even be preferred—at least by me. You should have no inhibitions about choosing whatever chords or alternates you may prefer for whatever reasons: musical or ease of finger positioning.

I added a category called Common Flat Key Chords because although *flat* keys are not preferred by guitarists (for reasons too technical to go into here), there are certain flat chords you should be able to play. I listed the most common ones.

I didn't categorize ninth, eleventh, thirteenth, or augmented chords because seventh chords of the same letter designation can almost always be substituted.

Above all, since you will see guitar chords diagrammed many different ways, you should feel free to decide for yourself whether or not to strum certain strings, or what fingering to use, regardless of the markings. For example, in the basic G chord it is obvious that you should strum the second, third, and fourth open strings even when they aren't marked with an *o*. Similarly, you may prefer to strum the fifth string in some D chords, or the sixth in some A chords even though they may be marked with an *x*. So let your personal taste be your guide when choosing and using the following chords.

Basic Major Chords

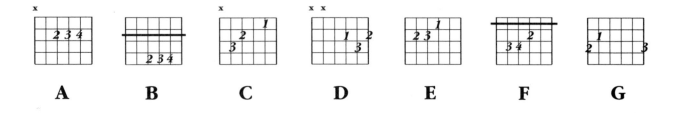

Dominant Seventh Chords

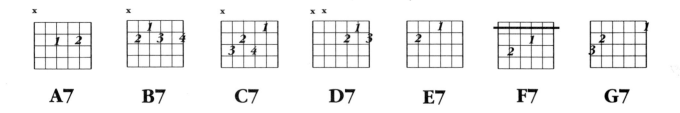

Minor Seventh Chords

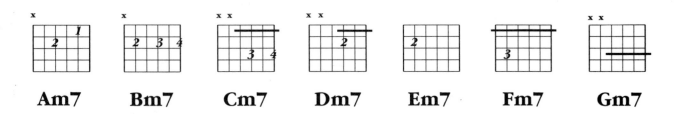

Minor Chords

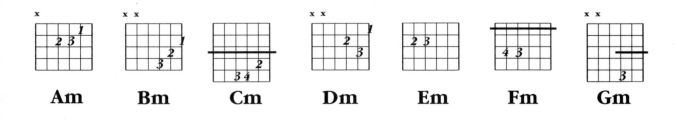

Minor Sixth Chords

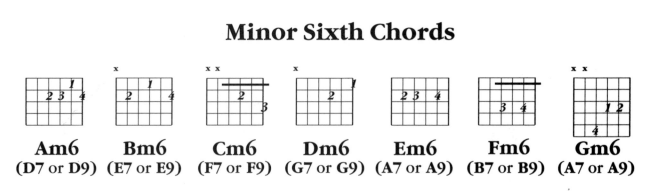

Am6
(D7 or D9)

Bm6
(E7 or E9)

Cm6
(F7 or F9)

Dm6
(G7 or G9)

Em6
(A7 or A9)

Fm6
(B7 or B9)

Gm6
(A7 or A9)

Chords in parentheses often may be used as substitutes for positional and/or musical reasons, even though they don't have the same notes, as in the case of minor sevenths and major sixths.

Major Sixth Chords

A6 **B6** **C6** **D6** **E6** **F6** **G6**

Major Seventh Chords

AM7 **BM7** **CM7** **DM7** **EM7** **FM7** **GM7**

Suspended Seventh Chords

A7sus4 **B7sus4** **C7sus4** **D7sus4** **E7sus4** **F7sus4** **G7sus4**

Diminished Seventh Chords

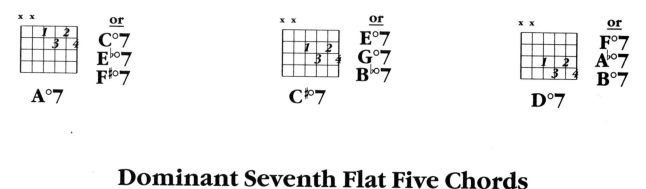

A°7	**or** C°7 E♭°7 F♯°7	C♯°7	**or** E°7 G°7 B♭°7	D°7	**or** F°7 A♭°7 B°7

Dominant Seventh Flat Five Chords

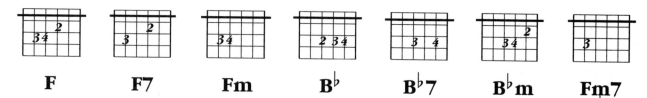

A7♭5 E♭7♭5	B7♭5 F7♭5	C7♭5 F♯7♭5	D7♭5 A♭7♭5	E7♭5 B♭7♭5	F7♭5 B7♭5	G7♭5 D♭7♭5

Dominant seventh flat five chords have the same notes as other dominant seventh flat five chords and may substitute for one another.

Basic Bar Chords

F	F7	Fm	B♭	B♭7	B♭m	Fm7 A♭6

All the above bar chords may be fingered as well as produced by a capo by the beginner after a minimal amount of practice. Each time the bar is moved to the next higher fret, the next higher note in the scale will apply. Thus, moving the first F bar chord up one fret will produce an F♯ (or G♭) chord, ect. Therfore, mastering these bar chords will make it possible for you to play a great number of chords in relatively easy finger positions.

Common Flat-Key Chords

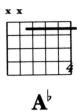 **A**♭

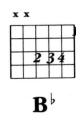 **B**♭

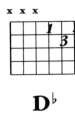 **D**♭

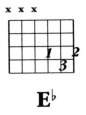 **E**♭

 A♭**m**

 B♭**m**

 D♭**m**

 E♭**m**

A♭**7**

B♭**7**

D♭**7**

E♭**7**

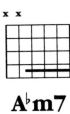 **A**♭**m7**

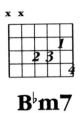 **B**♭**m7**

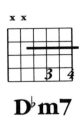 **D**♭**m7**

 E♭**m7**

BASIC JAZZ CHORDS

The following 12 chords are the ones most widely used for songs of the Big Band era as well as most modern jazz. Whether you wish to play the songs written by Gershwin, Rodgers, or Porter; those played by Marian McPartland, George Shearing, or Billy Joel; or those sung by Ella Fitzgerald, Mel Torme, or Frank Sinatra, these are the chords you need to know to do justice to the music. They may seem a bit difficult at first, but with patience, and after you have learned the previous popular chords, you should be able to manage them to your satisfaction.

The *x* above the diagrams, as you know, means that particular string should not be struck. The *m* above the diagrams (not those in the chord symbols) stands for *muffled*, or *muted*. Strings marked that way should be touched lightly by neighboring fingers but not pressed hard enough to make a sound. For example, in producing the third chord (Am7), your third finger forms a bar over the first four strings while your second finger not only presses the fifth fret of the sixth string but leans lightly enough against the fifth string to mute it. Test this by strumming each individual string so that every string produces a tone except the fifth.

In some cases I have added alternate symbols; for example, the second chord, Em7, may sometimes serve as a G6, depending upon the context in which it is used.

As in the case of the popular bar-chord positions previously shown, these jazz chords may be moved up (and in some cases down) the frets provided that the *x* and *m* marks are observed. Therefore, once you know how to play these chords you will be able to play many, many more chords in different keys.

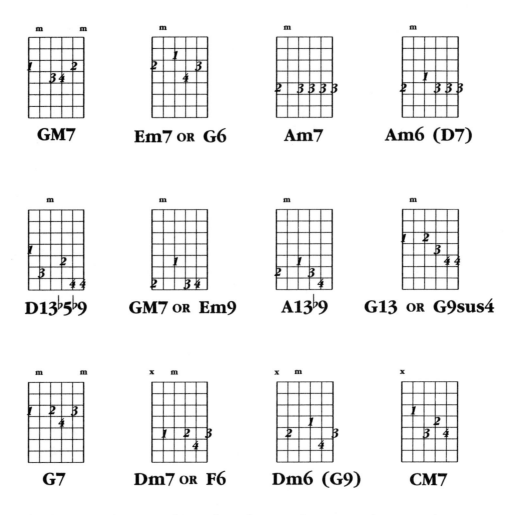

GM7   Em7 OR G6   Am7   Am6 (D7)

D13♭5♭9   GM7 OR Em9   A13♭9   G13 OR G9sus4

G7   Dm7 OR F6   Dm6 (G9)   CM7

*Chords in parentheses may be used as substitutes for positional or musical reasons.

MUSIC NOTATION

Music for the guitar is written on a staff consisting of five lines and four spaces, as you've seen on the lead sheets in this book. Also, for convenience, guitar music is written on a treble-clef staff, which is indicated by the treble-clef symbol:

Spaces   Lines

G
(where the treble clef symbol begins— or ends—when drawn)

E F G A B C D E F   F A C E   E G B D F

Treble Clef (or G Clef).

This staff indicates which notes are Cs, Ds, Es, etc., by their placement on the lines and spaces. Since the treble-clef symbol marks the location of the note G, on the second line, it is also called the G clef.

As you can see, the notes on the spaces spell FACE, an easily remembered acronym. The lines, EGBDF, are often remembered by the phrase Every Good Boy Does Fine. Notes that fall below or above the five lines and four spaces can be designated by *leger* lines—extensions of the regular staff that create additional lines and spaces. Here are some leger-line notes below and above the staff:

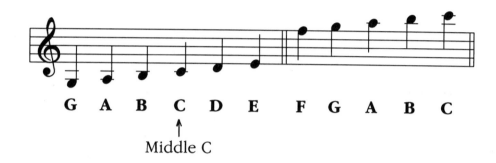

G   A   B   C   D   E   F   G   A   B   C

Middle C

Obviously, notes that fall far below or above the staff would require too many leger lines to be easily read. Music that requires such notes is written on staffs headed by other clefs than treble, such as bass or tenor clefs. However, we need not be concerned with those clefs with respect to guitar music.

The diagram on page 25 shows the actual notes to which a guitar is tuned and how they correspond to the keys of a piano. While the note G below middle C is readable on a treble-clef staff, the D below it would require too many leger lines. It would look like this:

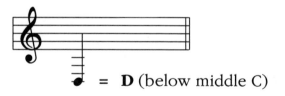

= **D** (below middle C)

Therefore, to make it easier to read notes on treble clef—the clef that is used for the vocal lines in sheet music and fake books—notes for guitar are written an octave higher than they actually sound. So the above D would appear this way:

When pianists play the notes as written on a lead sheet, they are said to be playing them *in concert*—meaning they sound exactly as written. Guitarists are playing them so that they sound an octave lower, a fact you should know although it is rarely relevant.

All the notes shown thus far are *natural* (♮) notes. That is, they are neither *sharps* (♯) nor *flats* (♭), both of which are called *accidentals*. The best way to describe and define all such notes is to show how they relate to the keys of a piano, which uses the letters A through G. (The standard piano has eighty-eight keys, including seven Cs, the one closest to the middle being referred to as middle C.)

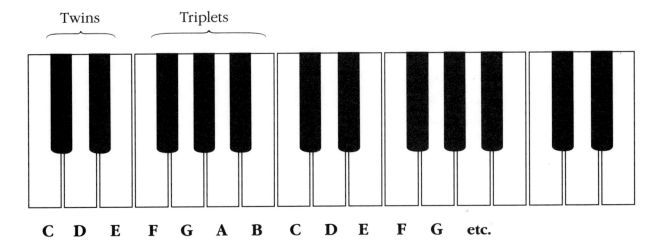

As you can see, notes on the piano are both black and white, the black ones appearing in groups referred to as *twins* and *triplets*. All notes on the keyboard, whether black or white, are considered to be a half tone (also called a semitone or a half step) apart. Thus, the black notes between the Cs and Ds are one half tone apart from the surrounding Cs and Ds, and the notes E and F are one half tone apart even though both are white keys. The black notes derive their names from their neighbors. For example, the black notes immediately to the right of the Cs may be called C♯ (C sharp) or D♭ (D flat). (To sharp a note is to raise its pitch; to flat it is to lower its pitch.)

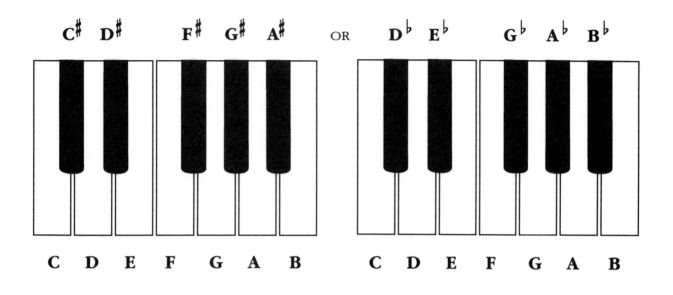

Whether a black note is considered to be a sharp or a flat depends on the context of the music and is not relevant at this point. What matters is that you know which notes are which, however they are depicted.

These two staffs show the same nine notes, whether played on a piano or a guitar. The natural (♮) signs in the staff on the bottom negate the flat (♭) signs on the preceding note of the same letter. (Once a note is sharped or flatted, it remains so in any given measure until it is *naturaled*.) Thus, if you wanted to show middle C followed by C sharp and back to middle C, the natural sign would be used in this manner:

Some melodies are written in keys in which most of the notes are natural. Others are in keys in which specific notes may appear mostly as flats or sharps. For example, the *key signature* of "Clementine" (page 69) is:

This means that the note B, wherever shown, must be B♭ unless accompanied by a natural sign. Thus, in the following example, all three Bs would be played as B♭s:

Key signatures eliminate the necessity of indicating numerous sharp and flat signs in songs where many notes are sharped or flatted throughout. Here are the key signatures for the most-used keys in which popular songs are written:

Key of Song	Key Signature	
C		No sharps or flats
G		F is sharped
D		F and C are sharped
A		F, C, and G are sharped

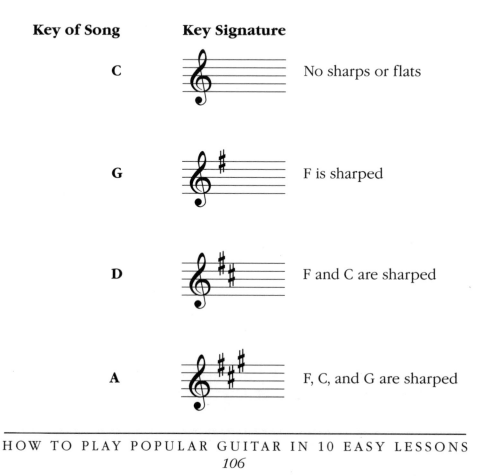

Key of Song	Key Signature	

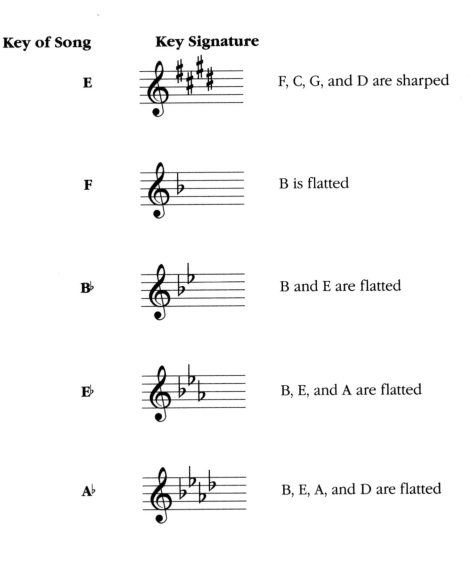

E		F, C, G, and D are sharped
F		B is flatted
B♭		B and E are flatted
E♭		B, E, and A are flatted
A♭		B, E, A, and D are flatted

If you're wondering why the key of C has no sharps or flats in its key signature while the key of E has four sharps, here's the quickest explanation I can give: most of our popular as well as classical music is based on the *diatonic* major scale. That is the scale you create when you sing "*Do re mi fa so la ti do.*" If you played C, D, E, F, G, A, B, and C on the piano or electronic keyboard, you would be producing a diatonic major scale—and you would be playing only the white notes.

Earlier I mentioned that all keys on the piano are considered a half tone apart, regardless of their color. The formula for establishing a diatonic major scale in terms of tonal distances, or *intervals*, is 1, 1, 1/2, 1, 1, 1, 1/2. For example, in the C major scale, D is a full tone apart from C, and E is a full tone apart from D. But the next interval is a half-tone, and since the white note F is adjacent to the white note E, it fulfills the requirement to be the next note. Thus, the formula in the key of C results in all *natural* notes—no sharps or flats. However, if you begin on the note G to form a major scale, you will have to play an F♯, not F♮, to fulfill the formula.

Since the piano keyboard is used as the basis for determining key signatures, you will almost never see a B♯ or a C♭ or an E♯ or an F♭. Because they are white notes, B♯s are simply written as Cs and E♯s are written as Fs. That's why in the diagram on the opposite page, Bs are followed by Cs—not B♯s—and Es followed by Fs—not E♯s.

This diagram can be used for quick reference to locate a particular note on a particular string. (After the twelfth fret, the sequence begins again.) Some notes may be found on three different strings; for example:

This D may be played on the tenth fret of the sixth string, the fifth fret of the fifth string, or the open fourth string.

Your choice of which string to play a given note will depend upon what may precede and/or follow that note. In some cases you may prefer the sound of a fingered note to one on an open string. Therefore, it is helpful to familiarize yourself with certain notes so you can find them reasonably quickly. A good way to begin is to learn all the notes on a particular position mark if it were barred. For example, if the strings of the third fret were barred, the notes would become G, C, F, B♭, D, and G, from the sixth string to the first. Once you've become familiar with third-fret notes, you might try remembering those on the fifth fret. Obviously, the easier it becomes for you to locate notes on the guitar, the easier it will be for you to play melodies from a lead sheet.

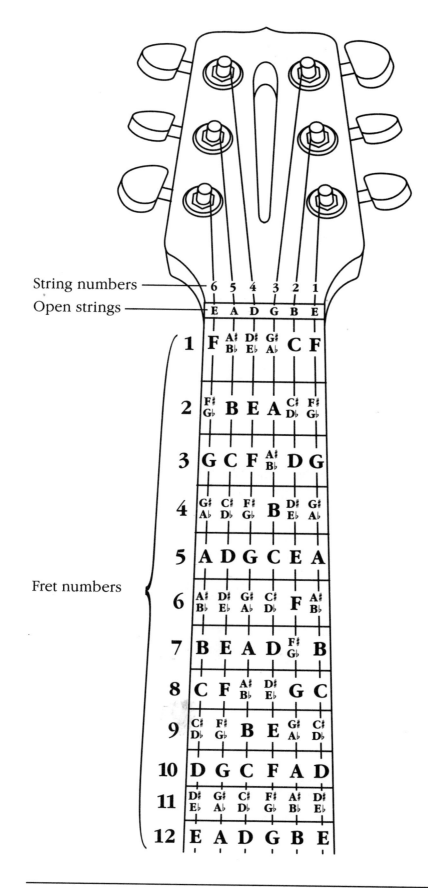

String numbers
Open strings
Fret numbers

HOW CHORDS ARE FORMED

In Lesson 8 you learned about the tonic, subdominant, and dominant—or the one, four, and five—chords. The best way to explain these references in greater detail is to begin with the diatonic major scale. Here is that scale in the key of C, showing the one, four, and five notes and the chords they produce:

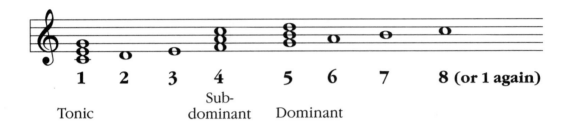

The chords formed on the one, four, and five notes are the most widely used chords in popular music. If those were the only chords you knew, you could play thousands of songs. As a matter of fact, you could play "To All the Girls I've Loved Before" using just the G, C, and D7 chords—the one, four, and five chords in the key of G. Instead of playing the Am7 chords, you can substitute the D7 chord, particularly if you use a thumb bass and brush strum. Here is the major scale in the key of G, once again showing the one, four, and five chords. However, in this example I have added the additional note to the five chord that changes it from a simple D major chord to a dominant seventh. (The additional note in *dominant* sevenths is always one and a half tones above the note under it, as will be explained later.)

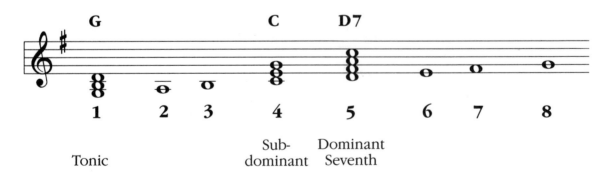

Note that the key signature of G indicates that all Fs are to be sharped (unless followed by ♮, the natural sign). Therefore, the D7 chord shown above is made up of the notes D, F♯, A, and C. As you have already learned, there are different kinds of seventh chords: the dominant seventh, the minor seventh, the diminished seventh, the suspended seventh, the augmented seventh, and altered sevenths such as D7♭5, for example. To understand how these and other chords are built requires an understanding of how the simple major chord—or *triad*, because it has only three notes—is formed.

In all simple major chords, the second note is two full tones apart from the first note, and the third note is a tone and a half apart from the second; in other words, the formula is 2 and 1½. If you look at the C scale on page 110 you'll find the C chord is made up of the notes C, E, and G—E is two tones higher than C, and G is one and one-half tones higher than E. The same intervals apply to the F and G chords shown on that page. Thus, following that formula, an E chord would be made up of E, G♯, and B; an A chord would be made up of A, C♯, and E; etc. Also, as long as you play the notes C, E, G or E, C, G or G, C, E, you will be playing a C chord. When the key note of the chord is not the starting, or bass, note, you are playing an *inversion* of the chord. Inversions are often used on pianos as well as guitars for positional reasons—the ease of the fingers—as well as for subtle differences in sound.

Using the simple major chord as a base makes it easy to explain how different chords are formed. The three notes of the major chord are the first, third, and fifth notes. To change any chord from major to minor you simply lower the third by a half tone. Thus, Cm would consist of C, E♭, and G, the E having been flatted, or lowered, by a half tone. Fm would be F, A♭, and C; and the A chord would have a C natural, not a C♯, as its third in order to become Am.

To diminish a chord, lower the fifth as well as the third, so C° (Cdim) would consist of C, E♭, and G♭; Gdim would be G, B♭, and D♭. To augment a chord, simply raise the fifth by a half tone: C, E, and G♯ or F, A, and C♯, etc.

To form the various seventh chords, use the *dominant* position as the base: that is, a simple major triad plus a note we add that is one and a half tones above the fifth. Thus, the D7 on page 110 consists of D, F♯, A, and C. To change D7 to Dm7, lower the third, F♯, to F♮; so Dm7 is D, F, A, C. Gm7 is G, B♭, D, F. To diminish a seventh chord, use the same principle: starting with the dominant form, lower the seventh as well as the third and fifth. Thus, Cdim7 consists of C, E♭, G♭, and A.

The formula for augmenting a seventh chord is the same as the formula for augmenting a major triad: raise the fifth by a half tone. Thus, Caug7 has a G♯ instead of a G natural, resulting in C, E, G♯, B♭. A suspended seventh means raising the third by a half tone; so a Csus7 chord would be C, F, G, B♭ instead of C, E, G, B♭. And a C7♭5 means lowering the fifth—flatting it—so the notes would be C, E, G♭, B♭.

The last seventh we need to explain is the *major* seventh, which is made up of the first, third, fifth, and seventh notes of the scale, the scale being determined by the first, or root note, of the particular seventh. Thus CM7 would be C, E, G, B; GM7 would be G, B, D, F♯ (F♯ being the seventh note in the G major scale according to the diatonic formula).

The reason we chose the dominant seventh rather than the major seventh as the model for forming all the other sevenths is this: lowering the third in a major seventh doesn't make it a minor seventh; raising the fifth in a major seventh doesn't make it an augmented seventh; but making those changes using the dominant form as the base does result in those changes. So once you become familiar with the dominant seventh form, changing to the other sevenths becomes easy.

Composers, at their creative best, have a way of surprising us with their unexpected use of chords. But creativity and a thorough understanding of chord structures go hand in hand. Nevertheless, there are certain conventional guidelines worth knowing regarding relationships among chords.

You have already studied numerous examples of how the dominant sevenths lead to the tonics of their respective keys—how G7 leads to C, D7 leads to G, and E7 leads to A, for example. However, it is quite common for the tonics themselves to become dominant sevenths leading to other tonic-dominant sevenths: G7 to C7 instead of C, D7 to G7 instead of G, and so on. In many songs you will find a series of dominant sevenths following that pattern—for example, E7 to A7 to D7 to G7 and perhaps finally to C. That pattern is referred to as the "circle of fifths" because the roots of the chords are a fifth apart in descending order: C is a fifth lower than G, so G7 leads to C; G is a fifth lower than D, so D7 leads to G. The next time you come across a series of dominant sevenths in a song, they will most likely be following the circle-of-fifths pattern.

Minor sevenths often follow a similar pattern, often preceding *dominant* sevenths as well as minor sevenths. The Am7 to D7 to G progression in "To All the Girls I've Loved Before" is a short example of that sequence (D is a fifth lower than A and G is a fifth lower than D).

Diminished sevenths are transitional chords, often acting as bridges. As such, they create an air of expectancy that resolves when the transition is completed. For example, in "Clementine" on page 39, you can play a C♯dim7 (as diagrammed on page 99) instead of a C, on the third syllable of "ex—ca—va—ting" before the G7 on the word "mine." (You can do the same on the third "darling" before the G7 on the third syllable of "Clem—en—tine.") In this case the diminished seventh is a bridge between C and G7 chords. A long interval between two chords can often be filled by a diminished seventh just before the second chord.

The easiest seventh chord to explain is the suspended seventh. As the name implies, it creates a feeling of suspense, which is resolved by following it with its namesake *dominant* seventh: C7sus to C7, D7sus to D7, etc. Try the following two examples (the letters above the diagrams are the notes of the chords):

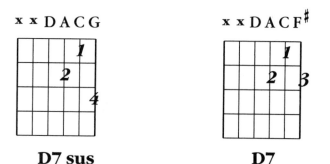

x x D A C G

D7 sus

x x D A C F♯

D7

The notes of D7 chord are D, F♯, A, and C. The G in the D7sus is resolved by the F♯ in the D7 chord.

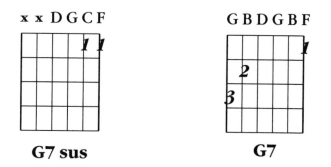

x x D G C F

G7 sus

G B D G B F

G7

The notes of G7 chord are G, B, D, and F. The C in the G7sus slips into a B in the G7 chord.

Suspended chords are often written as C7sus4 or D7sus4 because instead of the intervals being root, third, fifth, and seventh—as in dominant seventh chords—the intervals are root, *fourth*, fifth, and seventh. Going from the fourth to the third relieves the suspense of the suspension, so to speak.

Index